HERB
Gardens of Delight

*With Plants for Every Mood
and Purpose*

by Adelma Grenier Simmons

Drawings by Kathleen Bourke

To all Caprilands' gardening men, past and present, and all my assistants in plant selection, design and maintenance.

ACKNOWLEDGMENTS

The author wishes to thank Katie Bourke for the careful and inspired drawings; Helen Wilson for constantly stirring the author into action and seeing the projects through; and Liga Harrison for her reports on experiments with plant dyes.

For years **ADELMA GRENIER SIMMONS**, known far and wide as an author and lecturer deeply versed in every aspect of herbs—their lore, their culture, their practical and ornamental uses—has been developing Caprilands, her unique property in North Coventry, Connecticut, in many interesting ways. Here every year she revives the festivals associated with herbs, especially those of Christmas, entertains parties of guests with her gourmet cooking and her stories, guides groups around her fascinating gardens that are based on history and uses of herbs from medieval to modern times, and demonstrates in the Bouquet and Basket Shop the making of herbal wreaths, swags, and basket decorations.

"What I so much want," says Mrs. Simmons, "is to make gardeners aware of the historical significance of herbs and their uses and the great pleasure that awaits those who grow them."

Typography by Ellen Gal
Jacket Art by Katie Bourke

Contents

[vii]

Contents

GARDENS THROUGH HISTORY

THE VERSATILE HERB

Introduction: Gardens in Patterns

THE JOY OF GARDEN PLANNING is inherited from the great and humble gardeners of the past. Spread out before me as I write are two eighteenth-century engravings—one of Versailles, another of Fontainebleau. They lie on the crowded writing table close to the geometric fantasies of Château Chenonceau and the balanced beauties of Hampton Court. Nearby are photographs and drawings of the architectural masterpieces of Italian palace gardens and villas with their ancient statues and potted trees. Here also are knots and parterres of boxwood and yew, grand alleys, gushing fountains, and quiet lakes on which majestic swans make ripples on the silver surface.

Along with all this awesome beauty are simple dooryard plantings enclosed by old board fences where hollyhocks are tall and haughty, and lilacs familiarly brush the weather clapboards of eighteenth-century cottages. There are secluded spots where espaliered fruit trees line sunny walls and worn gates lead to secret trysting places of another time and world. There bees hum around skeps, beehives of yellow straw, in beds of roses bordered with thyme, and simple plantings surround old millstones or sundials mossy with age—places where the rushing of events is halted and time stands still.

Garden design inevitably becomes a part of the herb gardener's life. The enthusiasm for growing herbs leads to a study of the gardens of the past. No matter how small or how extensive the planting may be, the desire to place our treasures in the best way sends us poring through old books and new to find solutions for our problems. The seventeenth and eighteenth centuries are particularly rich periods for study. Even the tremendous designs of that period contain patterns that are applicable to the small plot and suit the modern do-it-yourself gardener.

American herb gardeners owe their most immediate debt to English settlers who brought with them seeds, plants, and memories of the gardens of their homeland. But the British, too, inherited much of their gardening skill and know-how.

The Roman conquerors were ardent horticulturists, farmers, and gardeners, and their villas reflected these interests. Their building of roads and towns was followed by plantings that fit the climate and the natural vegetation of the areas of their conquest. Plants native to the south of Europe found their way into the colder climates of Germany, France, and England where many of them naturalized.

The Romans bequeathed to the gardens the mount, an artificial heap of earth that was set in a strategic spot on which a summer house could be built or a place made for a watchman to observe the terrain. The building gave character and perspective to large gardens.

Topiary was another decorative device that came from the Roman gardens and took hold in England. Trees were trimmed into quaint and fantastic shapes—animals, birds, soldiers. They added interest to gardens that did not contain many flowers.

After the fall of the Roman Empire, systematized gardening in England disappeared or retreated into the monasteries and convents. For about a thousand years, from 400 to 1400, plants flourished and knowledge was preserved behind these walls.

The castle garden of this unsettled period was a small out-of-door living room where the medieval lords and ladies could escape the crowding, the smoke, and the evil odors of the castle. They could step from this atmosphere into the sunshine and flowers of the garden for pleasure and recreation. This pleasance was laid out within high brick walls at a distance from the castle. Entrance to it came through small locked gates, one from the castle and the other from the fields or the orchard. The pleasance was semicircular in shape. In the center was a fountain that did double duty as an attractive decorative piece and sometimes as bath or shower.

There were walks of sand that were held in place with stones, tiles, or often with animal bones. Planting was scarce, as gardeners of this time believed that having many plants in the soil would take the strength from the trees. For this reason and no doubt for the ease of moving, plants were grown in pots. Grass was generally not scythed, but was allowed to grow and produce wild flowers. People sat on the ground or on seats made of turf and planted with sweet-smelling herbs like thyme and camomile. The arbors, latticed fences, and alleys of fruit trees furnished the privacy that the great communal halls of the castles did not afford. The garden was the meeting place for lovers and friends, away from the castle's confusion.

Bowling greens and archery fields were common features of

fifteenth-century gardens. Men played games here while the women wove garlands. One young man of that day wrote his wife, "Know that it does not displease, but rather pleases me, that you should have roses to grow and violets to care for, and that you should make chaplets and dance and sing."

In the sixteenth and seventeenth centuries the sparsely planted beds of the medieval castles developed into elaborate designs called knots. or parterres. These were a sophisticated scheme of garden arrangement largely invented by the French. Knots were perhaps a development of the medieval maze, which was a low planting, formed of boxwood or yew, so arranged that once in it, it was difficult to get out. The maze and labyrinth trace their lineage to pre-Christian days, to the Egyptian Isis and the Eleusinian mysteries.

In the affluent times of Henry VIII and Queen Elizabeth I, the gardens of England reached their peak, although most of the influences on gardening were foreign. The great plantings of Cardinal Thomas Wolsey's development at Hampton Court and Whitehall, which later became Henry's domain, were developed under French influence and were planted by a French gardener. Elizabeth's gardens at Nonsuch were patterned, prettily French, and planned for the parading of the court out of doors. The patterns made an elaborate setting for the intricate clothing worn by members of the court.

The gardens of the Stuart kings were more Italian than English. They contained water gardens and semicircular summer houses. Theobalds, the garden of Lord Burghly, was made even more awesome by the inclusion of statues of twelve Roman emperors.

England gradually developed her own style for the gardens of the great manors, the noble houses, and the royal preserves. A plan for the rich country gentleman was advanced by Sir Francis Bacon in 1625 in his famous essay "Of Gardens." The princely estate described by Bacon was a square of not less than thirty acres. Four acres were set aside for an entrance and lawn, six were in heath or wild meadow, eight in side walks, and twelve were reserved for the main garden. Walks were an important feature, the main one being wide enough to accommodate four persons walking abreast. The side paths were arched over with the woven branches of hornbeam and willows and limes, and foot paths were of sand, gravel, or turf or were planted with low-growing herbs like camomile.

It was in the middle of the seventeenth century that the knot garden became popular in England. The knots were large, most of them occupying a 25-to-100-foot square and clearly intended for the rich man. Toward the end of the seventeenth century, paving stones and brick paths became the fashion. Posts were raised in the garden to act as stands for hand-carved animals, often heraldic in nature. Disks of gilded or colored glass were suspended from stakes and poles to glitter among the flowers. Lead ornaments were mounted on posts, and portrait busts and statues also populated the garden.

Elegant living was briefly interrupted by the puritanical Oliver Cromwell and the rise of the Commonwealth, but it was quickly regained with the return of Charles II from French exile. There were more furnishings for out-of-door living. Sundials, elaborate fountains, large flowerpots, and much statuary enhanced the gardens. The orangery, designed for winter housing of tropical plants, doubled as a protected living room in winter. Great architects, like Inigo Jones and Sir Christopher Wren, made drawings for these buildings which graced the great estates.

Though Cromwell's days saw a low ebb in gardening on a luxurious scale and the wholesale destruction of established plantings, they gave rise to a new look at practical farming. The small farmhouse became important during this period, and eventually there emerged small and cozy walled gardens that combined the growing of herbs, flowers, fruit trees, and vegetables.

One of the principal duties of the seventeenth-century housewife, from the meanest cottager to the lady of the manor, was the making of aromatic waters, home medicines, and cosmetics from the garden and the fields. Lavender water was first concocted and used in France, but it became so popular in England that few remembered its origin. For many years England had considered flowers a part of house and public sanitation. The floors of homes and public places were strewn with sweet-smelling herbs, and all English gentry reveled in perfumed baths. Judges in Old Bailey carried nosegays to court to protect themselves from jail fever, and the heads of canes were made hollow so they could be filled with herbs and spices. Sometimes pomanders (oranges stuck with cloves) topped the canes carried by doctors and others who visited the sick. The production of fragrances was very important in this period.

YOUR OWN HERB GARDEN

Planning and planting your herb garden should be a time of joy. Approach it with a sense of rare adventure, for that is what it will be. Learn the histories and legends of the plants you grow and you will savor some of the plant hunter's and the antiquarian's delights. Learn about the plants dedicated to the Virgin Mary and the saints and cherish them with the zeal of the religious approaching a shrine. Try your genius for creative design. Do an original or a traditional knot garden or a garden of symbolism. Be a gourmet and specialize in cooking herbs. Be a perfumer, growing your own fragrances. Or be a plain dirt gardener, sharing the common kinship of all who cultivate the soil.

Many of us start with only one of these gardener's attributes but acquire the others. Some never feel all this joy, but it is there for the digging—whether in the soil or in the pages of an herbal or a cookbook.

Fortunately for potential herb gardeners, these hardy little plants will grow to some degree under trying conditions. So take heart. Even if you don't have the proverbial green thumb or have

[6]

a gravel bank for a garden, follow a few basic rules and try your luck for flavor, for fragrance, and for fun.

Remember, particularly when the few herbs you have acquired look straggly and lost, or weak and pale, or overgrown and overrun, that it is almost impossible to produce a good garden in one or even two seasons. Make at least a three-year plan—a five-year one is even better—and don't get discouraged with a few failures. From the second year on you will have plants that need organizing and curbing. Find an inconspicuous spot where you can plant the excess, for you may need it to fill in any winter-killed spaces.

Wherever you plant, there are three requisites. They are (1) good drainage except for the mints, (2) sweet or alkaline soil except for sweet woodruff, and (3) sun. The well-drained soil can be sandy, gravelly, or even stony. Add some good compost to these soils and sprinkle them with lime once a year. Add a mulch in the hottest summer weather to protect the plant roots and to preserve some moisture. Mulch again, being careful not to smother the plants, to protect them from winter thawing and freezing. Some of the really hardy herbs will thrive between rocks and stones where other plants would wither.

Almost all herbs require at least two hours of sun each day, although I have had reasonable success on the northwest side of the house where only very pale sunbeams creep through for a few hours. So if your grounds are shady, don't despair. You can still have herbs. They will develop different growth habits and will probably lean, as mine do, reaching for the light. The taste may not be so strong, but it will be strong enough for most seasoning purposes. Although a southern exposure is preferred, my northside herbs look grateful for the extra shade and moisture in the hottest and driest weather.

Herbs will grow well in the straight rows of a vegetable garden. The Shakers, America's first commercial gardeners, found that plants were easier to transplant, cultivate, and harvest when planted in this manner. But tradition prescribes a patterned herb garden, and modern gardeners prefer plantings that are in harmony with their homes. Contrary to the accepted theory that an informal border of successive bloom is easy to maintain, we find it easier to care for a garden containing beds of individual plants, where borders mark the design and broad walks give the humblest plant a jewellike setting.

The Paths

Paths and walks may be of various materials. Gardeners in the South favor brick. In Shakespeare's England many of the walks were of crushed stone, and large and handsome flagstones made terraces that extended into the herb and flower plantings. You can do this, too. Carefully mowed and edged grass walks can be effective for plants of considerable size.

We have found fieldstone paths the easiest to obtain in our area and delightful when planted with fragrant thymes between the stones. Such a walk is not neat, for thymes overgrow quickly and cover an intended design. Since fieldstones are irregular, you cannot be prim in using them. They are informal and lend themselves to cottage plantings. They match the drainage stones that frequently surround eighteenth-century dwellings and are allied in color tones to old stone walls and grayed wooden fences.

For a neat and prim effect, where the plants are sharply outlined and the design emphasized, nothing is as practical as finely crushed granite. For this purpose, we like a product known as hen grits. This is easy for the part-time gardener to procure and to maintain. It is also inexpensive and is particularly good for plantings that do not exceed twenty by forty feet. For larger gardens, crushed stone is more economical. Many commercial products are too startlingly white, and frequently they glisten. Hen grits weather well and can be renewed easily with the addition of one or two bags of the mixture every year.

Naturally the same stone colors are not easily found in all areas. In Connecticut there is a wonderful, warm-toned mixture that contains a collection of small, pea-shaped rocks. It tends toward a reddish brown with enough quartz and slate to give it life and resembles the river gravel used to cover muddy driveways in times past. This is called mixed peastone and particularly complements weathered wood. It is of endless fascination to our younger visitors who fill little pails and their pockets with the various-colored stones.

Our problem some years ago was to find a material appropriate for a long driveway to our old black and red house. Most materials were too harsh in color or suggested the wrong period. The peastone solved our problem, as it has for many others who wished to achieve the same harmony of materials.

Plain stone paths, where no vegetation is desired, can be kept free of weeds with the application of a weed killer once each year. Choose a time when you will have no visitors, since the chemical is poisonous. Organic gardeners will dislike this method. For them we can only say that weeding is good exercise, and it seems to be the only other way to keep paths neat and clear. We once used salt in our driveways but found that thymes loved it and grew out of their fertile beds and into the salted area, defeating our purpose. If you learn about your weeds as carefully as you learn about your flowers and other garden plants, you will soon know which are annuals and which are perennials. Pull up the annual weeds before they seed and get out the perennials with a dandelion digger.

Edgings

One of the first questions to ask about a potential garden plan concerns the material that will make sharp divisions between plantings and paths. A good design is lovely at any time of year and worth keeping. From my library window I can look down on our fragrance garden, where even in winter the outline of the walks can be traced. The border of shrubby lavenders and the circular bed where small bushes of thyme surround the sundial stand out against the snow. These beds are edged with weathered wood that is slightly raised to provide good drainage. It is an attractive sight on a frigid February day.

Brick is the classic edging. Certainly it is the quickest of all materials with which to make an outline. Fieldstone, carefully chosen for good color and uniformity, is also quick and easy to apply.

Although wood is the least permanent of edging material, it is one of the most interesting to work with and will generally last as long as the first planting. All gardens have to be restored occasionally. We prefer weathered-wood barn rafters, and for large plantings, old beams that are not quite good enough for construction but will last for years along the herb plots. Since old wood is frequently warped, you will have to be selective about the pieces to be used for straight lines and may have to substitute something less ancient if you wish the plot to be as even as possible. To those of us who like the lack of uniformity in old materials, this is not a problem, and it can be overcome with clever planting. No matter how much you prize your edgings, herbs will never stay within them. Plants will need trimming about three times during the growing season if the design is to be maintained. Clippings can frequently be used in fresh and dried arrangements or in fragrant mixtures for sachets and rose jars.

Hedges and Fences

Old manuscripts and tapestries indicate that many of the early herb gardens were enclosed to provide privacy and to add to the beauty of the plantings. The walls were made of stone, or wood, or turf covered with thyme or camomile. Living fences were made of hawthorn, privet, eglantine roses, and firethorn. Today's fences of *Rosa chinensis* are good for large properties, but they are too coarse and spreading for small areas. Privet and barberry can, however, be kept neat and trim. Stockade fences are convenient substitutes for walls and are ideal for small plots that need privacy and a background. Some plain but practical metal fencing can be made decorative with the addition of an attractive gate of Victorian wrought iron that will give it character.

Garden Ornaments

No herb garden seems complete without a sundial. Of these one of the best of the modern reproductions is the type known as an armillary. It is one of the oldest designs, and its arrow gives an accent to low plantings. I often set sundials on tree stumps or rocks. This gives even a new dial an air of antiquity.

The bee skep is another meaningful ornament for the garden, reminding us that honey and its production were one of the reasons for growing herbs in quantity. Straw skeps deteriorate rapidly if left out in wet weather. We suggest a shelter built of old wood against a building, perhaps a lean-to, as a practical way to house the skeps and prevent their destruction.

Wooden shrines with one of the saints of gardens, preferably Saint Fiacre, make excellent focal points and add character to special types of plantings. The shrines should be set on posts or stone walls.

Birdbaths should be simple unless they are treasured pieces of some artistic merit. Plain cement shells and round baths soon become attractively mossed and weathered. I use black iron kettles in kitchen gardens. They are appropriate and effective.

Plant Markers

Plant markers always present a problem. Slate is our answer to the problem of where to inscribe a long quotation, as in the Shakespeare garden or the garden of the saints. These markers are painted with white "outside" house paint so they will last for several years, but even then it is best to bring them inside for the winter to insure longer service. The gray of the background is harmonious with old stone walls and paths of either white or gray stone. The markers are easy to read, yet they do not dominate the scene, except in early spring when many of the plants are small. Slate can be obtained from dealers in old wood, from house wreckers, or from quarries in some parts of the country. Quarries are especially helpful if you wish to use odd and uneven pieces for marking individual plants.

Signs of old and weathered wood are especially appropriate for colonial restorations. The letters may be burned or carved into the wood. The staves of old sap buckets make attractive markers. If you like to print, these may be marked with a commercial, moisture-proof pencil. They will last all through the season. The pencil strikes into the wood, and the type can easily be renewed.

Wooden spoons may be used for markers in the kitchen garden or wherever culinary herbs are planted. Plan to replace them every second year unless they are treated with a preservative. Shingles may be shaped, cut to size, and attached to pointed sticks that can be driven into the ground. These fit well in large, primitive plantings. A wash of barn or venetian red paint rubbed into the shingle or a stain of raw umber will make a better surface for lettering.

Now you are ready to study our garden plans and decide on the kind of herb garden you will grow. You will find that working with herbs has a special charm that lasts throughout the year. The calm beauty of the garden will make it a place for contemplation, and the delightful odors and tastes will occupy you during even the bleakest winter.

Gardens for
Many Purposes

1
A Garden of Fragrance

SEGREGATING FRAGRANT HERBS may seem unnecessary, for all herbs, without exception, are fragrant to someone. There are, however, enough that are distinctive for their outstandingly good **smells** to warrant making a special fragrance garden, even though people will not always agree on the best aromas. One of the prime reasons for a planting of this kind is to supply the ingredients for

[15]

potpourris, rose jars, sweet pillows, and sachets. Most of these have a base of either roses or lavender.

In our Caprilands fragrance garden we have hedges of roses as an outside border. The roses that produce sweet petals are the taller bush types that need space and full sun. Fieldstone walks separate the individual plantings, and the whole pattern is outlined by gray granite chip walks. The beds are raised above the walks with board siding.

The first bed is fan-shaped and divided into three sections. On one side are the pungent mints, mint geraniums, and the surpassingly sweet orange mint, which is reminiscent of cologne, bergamot, and other pleasant things. English black peppermint is the strong peppermint used for tea and candy, for cooling bouquets, and for aromatic mixtures. It is also marvelous to clear the head and the sinuses, and was once of great repute for scholars with lagging minds.

The center section is devoted to a few of our favorite scented geraniums. Here are three kinds of rose-scented geraniums: the old-fashioned rose geranium, 'Rober's Lemon Rose,' and 'Skeleton Rose.' These natives of South Africa are sweeter than roses and retain their odors much longer. They do not exude their scents, but must be brushed or crushed to give off their sweetness. The borders of this section include the spicy-scented cheddar pink, the velvety mint geranium and the low-growing nutmeg-scented, apple-scented, and 'Old Spice.' Many other scented geraniums might be included.

Lemon balm spreads through the adjoining section. We dry this for potpourris and suggest it for all who welcome the lemon scent. Lemon geraniums also grow here. They are like little trees with their crisp curled leaves that give off a sweet citrus odor when brushed.

In the center of the garden, lemon-scented southernwood makes a large, handsome, fine-foliaged bush. It has many branches for cutting and hanging against the moth and the flea or for the more obscure use of growing hair on a bald head. Southernwood is also used as a medicinal tea, but is grown here primarily for its rich fruitlike odor.

The most fragrant of the thymes grow around a small sundial that is placed on a decorative stone in a round bed: golden lemon, narrow-leaf French, gray and silver culinary thymes, creeping golden lemon, green lemon, and spicy-smelling Caprilands thymes. These thymes may be used in potpourris or just for smelling. We use narrow-leaf French and lemon thyme in potpourri but generally avoid those with the strongest odors, although they may be used in a medicinal-smelling herbal mixture.

The bed at the end of the center row is the home each year of a gigantic potted rosemary during the growing season. We have surrounded the big bush with small prostrate plants that make an excellent ground cover and blossom frequently. We cut these for use in herb and spice wreaths.

Sections of the beds on each side of the rosemary are planted with hardy lavenders that give off a sweet odor as one brushes against them, so that the odor is carried on into the house. The uses of lavender as a fragrance are well known. It is a symbol of cleanliness and virginity and once had a medicinal use for sunstroke. Included among the lavenders is a stunning bush of *Lavandula heterophylla*, a large plant that is almost continually in bloom. It has the sweetest-smelling foliage, equally good when dried, and is a stunning garden plant, but it must be wintered inside. Tender *L. dentata* is also included for its sweet foliage. In the fall the two back beds are interesting because of the salvias— *Salvia elegans*, with long red spikes of blossoms, and *S. leucantha*, with tremendous velvety purple blooms. These sages are both fragrant, although to many noses leucantha is not entirely pleasant. In the same beds, pinks, the carnation types called sops in wine because they were included in drinks, are a source of early summer scent and color. Bergamots, one red and one pale pink or almost white, furnish us with late summer color and scented leaves all season.

Lemon verbenas are set into the two saw-shaped beds. When

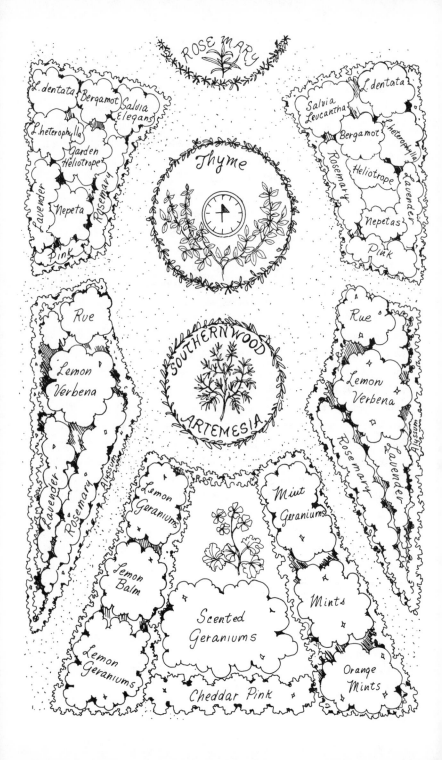

they are planted in early spring, usually in April, they are sorry-looking little sticks, and it seems that something like a miracle happens to turn them into stubby shrubs with hundreds of lemon-smelling leaves. They grow their best in very warm weather, for they remember their native home in the high mountains of Guatemala, Mexico, and South America, where the only snow is found on the mountain peaks and the warm sun shines all day.

Lemon verbenas must be wintered inside. They bitterly resent any change and drop their leaves in protest at moving time. I suggest that you collect these leaves and make a lemon potpourris with this windfall. Mix them with some lemon balm, a little dried lemon peel, and granulated orris root. Add some dried marigolds for extra color. Put this mixture into small glass apothecary jars and you will have excellent Christmas gifts. In the winter continue to water the leafless lemon verbena, and in March you will be rewarded with new leaves and signs of growth. Sometimes these temperamental plants will leaf out and drop their leaves again until they eventually put on their summer dress. For their unparalleled scent they are worth any amount of bother.

We leave this garden with a bouquet of interesting geranium leaves that may be used as bookmarks or tied into dried arrangements that will retain their fragrance for a year or more.

PLANTS FOR THE
FRAGRANCE GARDEN

Bergamot   *Monarda didyma*
Bee Balm   *M. fistulosa*

This fragrant plant gives off a citruslike odor that resembles the smell of oil made from a tropical tree of the same name. The purple, white, pink, and red flowers are excellent for cutting and for dried arrangements. We have used the pink- and red-flowering ones. The dried leaves are included in many potpourris recipes.

Garden Heliotrope   *Valeriana officinalis*
Valerian

Garden heliotrope is a sweet-scented medicinal herb. The root has been used to cure insomnia, to treat epilepsy, to soothe nerves, and to quiet heart palpitations. We include it in the fragrance garden for the heliotropelike scent of its clusters of pale pink flowers and as a reminder that Asians used its relatives for spices and perfumes.

Geraniums (*Pelargoniums*)

It would be difficult to imagine a fragrance garden without a selection of the marvelous pelargoniums we have adopted from the South African Cape. They are attractively shaped plants with variously scented leaves. The leaves of many kinds are also marked in interesting patterns. For convenience in selecting the plants for a particular bed or to be grown in combinations with other scented plants, we have grouped them by odor. In a few cases, some gardeners will not agree with these classifications, but those about which there might be serious disagreement have been indicated.

Geraniums with Earthy Smells

Giant Oak Geranium   *Pelargonium quercifolium* 'Giganteum'

Giant oak has large, coarse, three-to-five-lobed leaves that are marked in veins of deep purple. It is a rather rangy plant with sticky stems and leaves and small rose-colored flowers. The "earthy" smell reminds me of fallen leaves.

'Little Gem' Geranium   *P. graveolens* 'Little Gem'

'Little Gem' is very much like the old-fashioned rose geranium (*P. graveolens*) except the scent is more earthy than roselike. It makes an interesting border plant, since it is low-growing. 'Little Gem' bears many lavender rose flowers.

Prostrate Oak Geranium   *P. quercifolium* 'Prostratum'

Prostrate oak is a low-growing, prostrate, or trailing plant. It has five-lobed leaves with purple markings and small lavender flowers with purple veins. The scent suggests the odor of fallen leaves.

Fruit-scented Geraniums

Apple-scented Geranium   *P. odoratissimum*

Apple geranium should be in every garden. I plant it each year, alternating it with the similar but grayer 'nutmeg.' Bordering a walk, it maintains a trim appearance quite in keeping with the "proper" look of a border plant. It is fragrant to brush while walking by. The plant has light green, crenate leaves that are rather velvety. Tiny white flowers with red markings appear in early spring.

'Apricot' Geranium   *P. scabrum* 'Apricot'

'Apricot' geranium is a handsome plant with dark green, glossy leaves that are deeply cut. The rose-colored flowers are large with darker markings.

Gooseberry-leaved Geranium   *P. crispum* Gooseberry-leaved

The interesting ruffled leaves of this compact geranium are mottled green and yellow. The free-flowering, attractive plant is excellent for an accent in the foreground of a planting. The in-frequent flowers are pale lavender with darker markings. The leaves have a fruity scent.

'Lady Mary' Geranium   *P. limoneum* 'Lady Mary'

The lemon scent of 'Lady Mary' is very delicate. This compact plant has small, fanlike, hairy leaves. It is particularly interesting for its lovely magenta blossoms which are marked with carmine.

Lemon Balm Geranium   *P. melissimum*

Lemon balm smells faintly of lemon, but the scent is more pungent. It really smells like lemon balm. This is one of the most rapidly growing of the scented plants and, for that reason, is of special importance where height is desired, especially for a background. Its light green leaves resemble the maple leaf in shape. The lavender flowers are marked with purple.

Lemon-scented Geranium   *P. crispum*

The lemon geranium is second only to the old-fashioned rose geranium in the memories of those who attempt to reconstruct the gardens of the past. There are many varieties with this fresh lemon scent.

Lemon-scented Geranium   *P. limoneum*

Lemon geranium has the strongest lemony scent of its group. It has toothed, fan-shaped leaves and small lavender flowers.

Lime-scented Geranium   *P. nervosum*

Lime geranium has one of the most fragrant and refreshing odors of the fruit-scented group. There is no mistaking the odor. The plant is compact and covered with small, deep green, sharply dentated leaves and good lavender flowers.

Little-Leaf Rose Geranium   *P. graveolens* 'Minor'

The small leaves of this plant are cut like those of the graveolens group. The plant is covered with small orchid blooms in the spring and early summer. It stays compact with a little care. The odor is pleasantly lemony.

'Prince of Orange' Geranium   *P.* 'Prince of Orange'

'Prince of Orange' is a compact, small-leaved plant that will become large when full grown. It has the wonderful odor of oranges and freely produces rather pale lavender flowers with maroon markings.

'Prince Rupert' Geranium   *P. crispum* 'Prince Rupert'

During the space of one summer in the garden under even fair conditions this will become a small shrub. It has a strong lemony scent and is the most like an evergreen tree of all lemon-scented geraniums. It has small, smooth, crenate leaves and lavender flowers with carmine veins.

'Prince Rupert Variegated' Geranium

P.c. 'Prince Rupert Variegated'
This very distinguished small plant lives up to its royal name. Its ruffled green leaves are edged in white or yellow, and the lavender flowers have carmine veins.

Southernwood-leaved Geranium   *P. abrotanifolium*

The finely cut, grayish silver leaves of this plant so resemble those of the artemisia that it could easily be mistaken for one. The woody stems bear white flowers with carmine markings. The leaves have the scent of a very strong southernwood artemisia.

Geraniums with the Scent of Heavy Incense

The pungent scent of most of the oak-leaf geraniums (*P. quercifolium*) is strong and acrid, a little like a heavy incense. The scent lingers on your hands long after you have brushed the leaves. Sometimes these plants seem to be growing two or three kinds of leaves at the same time because there are marked variations between the old and the new leaves.

'Fair Ellen' Geranium   *P. quercifolium* 'Fair Ellen'

'Fair Ellen,' a trailing plant, has round-lobed leaves that are rough and sticky. Both the leaves and the stems are marked with purple, though the markings vary. The abundant lavender flowers of medium size will last well into the summer if the plant gets sun. The scent is of heavy incense.

'Staghorn Oak Leaf' Geranium   *P.q.* 'Staghorn Oak Leaf'

'Staghorn Oak Leaf' has finely cut leaves with narrow purple veins on a trailing or hanging plant. The medium-sized flowers are lavender. The scent is of incense.

Nut-scented Geranium

'Schottesham Pet' Geranium   *P.* 'Schottesham Pet'

This is one of the most desirable scented and flowering plants from every point of view. The beautiful and lacy foliage is a light, shimmering, and transparent green. The numerous, brilliant, rosy red blossoms are borne over a long period of time. The leaves are filbert scented.

Coconut-scented Geranium   *P. grossularioides*
(formerly *P. parviflorum*)

The coconut geranium appears to be very delicate, but it actually has a tenacious hold on life. It is a trailing plant that grows out of a crown of leaves. The interesting, tiny blooms are almost red.

Rose-scented Geraniums

Rose Geraniums   *P. graveolens*
'Attar of Roses' Geranium

The true rose-scented geranium is as sweet as a rose and much more lasting, for the leaves retain their odor for years. It is well to remember, however, that many varieties of this plant exist and not all are *sweet*; some, though smelling of rose, might best be described as pungent. As the leaves are all, at first glance, very similar, it is necessary to brush the plant to release the odor so you can properly identify it.

Pelargoniums with the strong rose scent are important sources of rose oils or essences and are grown commercially for the French perfume industry. For home use we can incorporate them in our herb gardens, where they will produce large, sweet-smelling leaves that can be used in jellies, tea, and cakes, as well as in potpourris.

'Attar of Roses' is a tall and handsome plant with lobed and ruffled leaves. The small flowers are an attractive rosy purple. The scent is not strong, but it is definitely rose.

'Clorinda' Geranium   *P.* 'Clorinda'

This brilliant flowering geranium has a distinct wild rose odor to me. It is a vigorous plant with trailing growth and lovely pink blossoms. If I had to confine myself to a few of the scented geraniums, 'Clorinda' would head the list.

Denticulatum Geranium   *P. denticulatum*

This dense and compact plant has finely cut, light green leaves that give the effect of a filmy mass. The small lavender flowers are marked with carmine. There seems to be some disagreement about the scent. To me it is rose, but some find it pine scented.

'Dr. Livingston' Geranium   *P.* 'Dr. Livingston'
'Skeleton Rose' Geranium   *P. radens* 'Skeleton Rose'

'Dr. Livingston', sometimes called 'Skeleton Rose', is a vigorous plant. It has seven-lobed, finely cut leaves with a lemon rose scent. The flowers are pale lavender.

'Gray Lady Plymouth' Geranium

P. graveolens 'Gray Lady Plymouth'

This rapid grower is sometimes called the best of the variegated rose geraniums. The deeply cut, gray leaves have a bordering line of white. 'Gray Lady Plymouth' is a good bedding plant; it bears numerous small orchid flowers with purple veins and has a good rose scent.

'Lady Plymouth' Geranium   *P.g.* 'Lady Plymouth'

'Lady Plymouth' is a small, variegated, almost white plant with finely cut leaves. Sometimes there is a tinge of pink on the leaves. The small orchid flowers are marked with purple. The rose scent is not quite so marked as it is in 'Gray Lady Plymouth'.

'Rober's Lemon Rose' Geranium   *P.g.* 'Rober's Lemon Rose'

This is one of the most fragrant plants for the scented garden. Its large thick leaf, which resembles the leaf of a tomato plant, holds enough fragrance for a whole garden of roses. The infrequent lavender flowers have darker markings on the upper petals. The scent could best be described as the name indicates.

'Skelton's Unique' Geranium   *P. quercifolium* 'Skelton's Unique'
    'Skelton's Unique' is a rangy plant with small, rather round leaves that are ruffled and hairy. The small arched blossoms appear in spring and summer. The scent is pungent, but rosy.

Spice-scented Geraniums

'Torento' Geranium   *P.* 'Torento'
Ginger-scented Geranium
    This rapidly growing plant has fan-shaped leaves and brilliant, rose lavender flowers. The scent is somewhat like ginger.

Nutmeg-scented Geranium   *P. fragrans*
    A solid border of nutmeg outlines our bed of scented geraniums. They grow exactly right to conceal the tall stalks of the many varieties behind them and unify the lines of the border, taking away that unkempt appearance that often comes with plantings containing a great number of shapes and sizes. The small plant has slightly lobed and crinkled, round, gray leaves and tiny white flowers. This is a highly scented trailing plant that is good for hanging baskets.

'Old Spice' Geranium   *P.f.* 'Old Spice'
    'Old Spice' has velvety leaves that smell of a medley of spices. The tiny flowers are marked with red.

Mint-scented Geraniums

'Beauty' Geranium   *P. quercifolium* 'Beauty'
    'Beauty' is excellent for wherever a large-leafed, low, and trailing plant is needed. It can also be trained as a climber. The "oak" leaves are very rough and marked with brown. The tiny rose

flowers are marked with purple. There is a hint of mint in the pungent odor.

'Joy Lucille' Geranium   *P.* 'Joy Lucille'
This is a rangy and procumbent plant with deeply cut leaves that are soft and downy. It has long, very pale lavender, almost pink, flowers. Most people find the odor reminds them of peppermint, but it makes me think of lilacs.

Peppermint-scented Geranium   *P. tomentosum*
The large, velvety, heart-shaped leaves of this mint geranium appear on procumbent branches. The tiny white flowers have inconspicuous purple markings. There is a somewhat medicinal peppermint odor to the leaves which combines well with the odor of the true mints in potpourris. They retain their shape well when dried.

'Snowflake' Geranium   *P. graveolens* 'Snowflake'
'Snowflake' grows to a tremendous size in the garden. The ruffly leaves become huge umbrellas filling ugly spaces very fast. They are light green blotched with white, the amount of white depending on cultural conditions. The small lavender flowers have purple markings, and the leaves have a pungent, minty rose odor.

Sweet-scented Geraniums

Blandfordianum Geranium   *P. blandfordianum*
The unusual gray, deeply cut leaves make this plant an interesting contrast with most other geraniums. The white flowers are marked with carmine. The scent is faintly sweet, with a suggestion of lemon.

Fern-Leaf Geranium   *P. denticulatum* Filicifolium
This tall and spreading plant has very finely cut, sticky leaves. Its tiny pink flowers are marked with carmine. The scent is sweet with a pungent undertone.

'Village Hill Hybrid' Geranium

P. quercifolium 'Village Hill Hybrid'

'Village Hill Hybrid' is an upright plant that grows fast and becomes so tall it could almost be called a climber. It has narrow, crenated leaves and bright lavender flowers marked with purple. This may be the most important member of the oak-leaf group. It has a sticky sweet, slightly medicinal odor.

Other Scented Geraniums

'Old Scarlet Unique' Geranium   *P.* 'Old Scarlet Unique'

A rare and handsome geranium with gray, woolly, and ruffled leaves that often have red edges and are tinged with scarlet. It is long-blooming, producing large scarlet flowers. The scent is very faint.

Pheasant's Foot Geranium   *P. glutinosum*

As the name implies, the leaves of this vigorous geranium are deeply cut. It is a rapid grower that makes a handsome background plant. The scent is heavy and medicinal, but pleasant.

'Rollisson's Unique' Geranium   *P.* 'Rollisson's Unique'

If given support, this tall and rangy plant will become a rampant climber. The leaves are large and slightly crinkled and the flowers a brilliant magenta. The faint scent is difficult to describe, but many find it slightly like mint.

Lavender   *Lavandula* varieties

Lavender is one of the most ancient fragrances. In early times it was used as a symbol of cleanliness and health. It was also reputed to be a preserver of virtue. The entire family is highly scented. Both the leaves and the blossoms are used, though the blooms give off the most odor and carry the characteristic color. Used in varying amounts, lavender will improve almost all potpourris. Sometimes it is useful for the color that it adds to a glass jar, or its clean odor may be the cool element needed to calm an overpowering mixture.

Lemon Balm   *Melissa officinalis*

Lemon balm has a delightful odor. It is attractive to bees and resembles lemon verbena but has the added advantage of wintering over outside. Its wrinkled leaf is especially decorative in the spring when it emerges from the ground. The oil is used in perfumes, and the dried leaves are most useful in potpourris.

Lemon Verbena   *Lippia citriodora*

The leaves of lemon verbena are very fragrant; indeed, there is no other odor quite like it. The attractive plants might be grown in tubs, for they must be wintered indoors. When they are outside, the leaves are dark and glossy. The dried leaves are invaluable for potpourris.

Mint (*Mentha*)

Apple Mint   *Mentha rotundifolia*

The soft, gray green, fuzzy leaves make this mint a charming, fragrant, and cooling addition to flower arrangements.

Orange Mint   *M. citrata*
Bergamot Mint

Orange mint is one of the most fragrant plants in the garden and is certainly the sweetest of the mints. The clean citrus scent combines well with lavender and bergamot, which it resembles in odor. It dries well, keeping a good green color.

Peppermint, English Black   *M. piperita vulgaris*

English peppermint is a very decorative plant with dark, reddish purple leaves. It is too strong for the sweet jars but is wonderful in a more medicinal-smelling mixture that can be used as one

[29]

uses menthol, which takes its name from *mentha*. Its prime value is to clear the head, and it can be used as the ancient scholars used the mints: to clear the brain.

Pineapple Mint   *M. rotundifolia variegata*
This mint is attractive enough as a border plant to be grown just for its beauty. The leaves are variegated green and white.

Spearmint   *M. spicata*
Because of its clean, fresh odor, this green-and-gold-flecked mint was used in baths in ancient times and as a strewing herb in medieval houses.

Nepeta   *Nepeta* varieties
The best known member of this decorative group of plants is catnip (*N. cataria*), but there are many other very attractive relatives. They belong to the mint family and most have grayish, hairy leaves. We like to grow *N. cataria*, with its dense spikes of pale purple flowers; *N. grandiflora*, for the blue flowers in loose racemes; *N. macrantha*, with clusters of blue flowers; *N. mussinii*, with blue or mauve flowers; and *N. nuda*, for its many-flowered racemes of violet to white flowers.

Pink, Cheddar   *Dianthus gratianopolitanus*
The showy rose flowers of this pink have a marvelous spicy scent. The flowers are attractive when dried or pressed, but they do not retain their odor for any length of time. A mat-forming plant that has slightly grayish leaves.

Rose   *Rosa centifolio*
                                                                         R. damascena
                                                                         R. moschata
R. centifolia bears solitary, very fragrant, pink double flowers on a four-to-six-foot shrub. *R. damascena* has clusters of red to pink double flowers on five-to-seven-foot plants. *R. moschata*, a

very tall, almost climbing, rose, bears white flowers in clusters. The flowers of *R. rugosa* are very large and either red or white. The shrub is usually between four and six feet high.

Rosemary   *Rosmarinus officinalis*
This most loved and cherished of all the herbs finds its way into every part of the gardener's life and appears in the culinary, the scented, and the legendary gardens. It goes into stews, stuffings, and gravies, wreaths, bouquets for brides, and potpourris. Rosemary has a spicy, gingery odor all its own. It sometimes appears in the garden in tubs because it must be wintered inside, but we also make a hedge of it bordering one side of the path leading to the house. These plants go directly into the ground but must be potted and brought in for the winter.

Rue   *Ruta graveolens*
Rue is an almost "evergreen" herb, with blue green leaves, clusters of yellow, starlike blossoms, and attractive red brown seedpods. It is an ornamental addition to any garden, but it is best placed where people will not brush it as they walk by, for it sometimes causes skin irritation. The whole plant has a strong odor when green, but the dried leaves are sweet and spicy.

Salvia, Sage   *Salvia* varieties
All salvias are desirable in the herb garden, but the blue-flowering ones are particularly appropriate, for they carry on the blue in the landscape after the lavenders have gone. Salvias have a long blooming period, and the flower heads dry well for potpourris.

Southernwood   *Artemisia abrotanum limoneum*
The artemisias are so attractive and have so many uses that one or another of them is a must in any herb garden. Almost all artemisias have lovely gray foliage that makes them most decorative. The southernwoods are particularly appropriate for fragrant

and decorative gardens; their name *abrotanum* means elegant in Greek, and that can refer to both scent and appearance. In our fragrant garden we include the lemon-scented southernwood for its aroma and for its finely cut, almost feathery, gray green leaves. Either the camphor-scented (*A.a. camphorata*) or the tangerine-scented (*A.a. procera*) might have been included. All of these are said to repel moths.

Thyme (*Thymus* varieties)

Many of the thymes seem fragrant enough for the potpourri. We use a little of narrow-leaf French thyme in our mixtures, as well as clippings of lemon thyme. We avoid those with the strongest and the most characteristic odors in our fragrant concoctions.

Golden Lemon Thyme   *Thymus serpyllum aureus*
The green leaves of this lemon-scented thyme are edged with gold. Each plant looks a bit like a miniature shrub.

Lemon Thyme   *T.s. vulgaris*
                                                  (*T.s. citriodorus*)
The deep green and shiny leaves of lemon thyme are both beautiful and fragrant. It grows higher than other serpyllums, so it makes an interesting and fragrant addition to flower arrangements.

Narrow-leaf French Thyme   *T. vulgaris* 'Narrow-leaf French'
French thyme is shrubby and grayish and bears small white flowers. The odor is sweeter than that of broad-leaf English thyme.

Silver Thyme   *T. serpyllum argenteus*
The variegation on the leaves of this shrublike thyme gives it a filmy look and a silvery cast. It makes an attractive bed by itself or in combination with the golden lemon and green lemon thymes. All their odors are quite sweet.

FRAGRANT RECIPES

The joy of a garden of fragrant herbs does not end with the first killing frost. That is the time to begin enjoying the stock of sweet-smelling leaves and flowers that were quickly dried and stored during the busy gardening months. Here are some pleasing recipes that will make the winter infinitely more enjoyable for you and for your friends who are lucky enough to receive a sachet or a potpourri for Christmas.

The ingredients used in these recipes can be obtained from:

> Aphrodisia Products, Inc.
> 28 Carmine Street
> New York, N.Y. 10014

> Caswell-Massey Co., Ltd.
> 518 Lexington Avenue
> New York, N.Y. 10017

> Caprilands Herb Farm
> Coventry, Conn. 06238

Spice Potpourri

Mix together these ingredients, ground fine or powdered:

> Rose petals, ¼ pound   Cinnamon bark, ¼ pound
> Sandalwood, ½ pound   Patchouly leaves, ¼ pound
> Musk, ¼ cup

Put in a bowl:

> Orris root, powdered, ½ pound

Add, mixing thoroughly:

> Sandalwood oil, 10 drops   Patchouly oil, 10 drops

Add mixture to petals and spices.

[33]

Sweet Woodruff Sachet

Sweet woodruff has long been used to drive away moths and to give a pleasant scent to rooms. Its small whorled leaves, emitting the sweetness of new-mown hay, can be used as a closet sachet without the addition of a fixative, or mixed with a little orris root and a ground vanilla bean for lasting fragrance.

Herb Sachet

This large recipe is an excellent way to use the overflow harvest of your herb garden. The sachet has a refreshing herbal odor that is not so sweet as the potpourris.

Crush, but do not powder, with a mortar and pestle or in a blender, the following dried leaves and spice:

Rosemary, 1 cup	Sweet marjoram, 1 cup
Thyme, 2 cups	Orange mint, 1 cup
Lemon verbena, 4 cups	Cinnamon sticks, 2
Lemon balm, 4 cups	

Grind into a powder and mix together:

Cloves, ¼ pound   Allspice, ½ pound

Add the spices to the leaves, along with the dried petals of:

Roses, 1 pound   Lavender, ½ pound

As a fixative, add to the mixture:

Orris root, granular (not powdered), ¼ pound

Lavender Sachet

This large recipe may be used alone as a sachet or as a base for a spice potpourri.

Place in a bowl these ingredients, ground into a fine powder:

Lavender flowers, 1 pound   Gum benzoin, ¼ pound

Mix together:

Orris root, granulated, ¼ pound   Oil of lavender, ¼ ounce

Mix thoroughly with the flowers.

Orange Potpourri

We make this potpourri after our holiday entertaining, when we have an accumulation of the peels of limes, lemons, and oranges used in festive punches. After the fruits are juiced, we scrape away the pulp and membrane from the peel to prevent mold, cut the peels into strips, and place them in a wire basket. They are then dried over a warm stove or in a slow oven, being stirred frequently. When the skins are crackle-dry, they are crushed to a powder in a grinder, or with mortar and pestle, or even with a rolling pin.

Place in a large bowl:

Ground citrus skins, oranges predominating, 2 cups
Orange blossoms, dried, 1 quart

Orange calendulas and orange marigolds, dried, enough for color
Leaves of orange mint and pineapple mint, dried, 1 quart

Add:

Granulated orris root, 1 cup
Orange blossom oil, 20 drops

Oil of bergamot, 10 drops
Oil of orange, 6 drops

Mix all together. Store in a tight container and allow to set for at least a week before using.

A Potpourri from the Saints' Garden

Mix together the dried leaves of:

Rosemary, 4 cups
Bay, crushed, 1 cup

Peppermint, spearmint, and lemon balm, mixed, 1 cup
Basil, ½ cup

Add:

Oregano, blossoms and leaves   Myrtle, leaves and shaved wood

Mix in the following ingredients, crushed:

Almond blossoms or bitter almonds	Cumin seed
	Cassia bark
Anise seed	Frankincense
Coriander seed	Myrrh

Rosemary Potpourri

This is the simplest of all potpourris. It will remain sweet, emitting fragrance from a large open bowl, for several months. For an indefinitely lasting fragrance, granulated orris root mixed with the essence of rosemary and lemon verbena can be added. For color you may add dried bachelor's buttons, pinks, and peony petals.

Mix together:

Rosemary clippings, 4 cups	Cinnamon sticks, ground, 4
Fresh lemon verbena leaves, 2 cups	Cloves, ground, ¼ cup

A Garden Potpourri

Put into a large bowl the dried leaves of:

Rose geranium, crushed, 1 quart	Apple mint, 1 cup
Lemon balm, 1 quart	Marjoram, 1 cup
Lavender, 1 quart	Lemon thyme, 1 cup
Thyme, vulgaris type, 1 cup	

Add the dried petals and buds of:

Roses, 1 quart	Musk, powdered, ¼ cup
Cloves, powdered, ¼ cup	Orris root, granulated, 1 cup
Allspice, powdered, ¼ cup	

Blend thoroughly.

Rose Geranium Potpourri

Prolific rose geraniums can be harvested throughout the summer or cut in large masses at the season's end. Hang them to dry in an airy room, not in direct sun. They dry very quickly. The leaves may then be removed from the stems easily. It is not difficult to get more than a quart of leaves from a single geranium. My favorite varieties for this mixture are 'Rober's Lemon Rose', the sweetest of the rose scents; 'Skeleton Rose'; and the familiar *Pelargonium graveolens*. A rose geranium potpourri can be made without essences and fixatives, although the leaves do have to be crushed to emit a strong scent.

Potpourri from the Shakespeare Garden

All the plants used in this potpourri are grown in the Shakespeare garden with the exception of eglantine, which is so large and spreading that we grow it along a bordering fence.

Mix together the following dried flowers:

Pinks, 1 cup	Johnny-jump-up
Lavender, 1 quart	(*Viola tricolor*), ½ cup
Iris, 1 cup	Violets, deep blue, 1 cup
Camomile, 1 cup	Hyssop, 1 cup
Pot marigold, 1 cup	Broom, 1 cup

Add the dried petals of:

Peony, 1 quart

Add the mixed dried leaves and little knotted flowers of:

Marjoram, 1 cup

To the mix of flowers add the dried leaves of:

Eglantine, 2 cups	Savory, ½ cup
Lemon balm, 2 cups	Thyme, 1 cup
Bay, 1 cup	Wormwood, ¼ cup
Mints, ½ cup	Rue, ¼ cup
Rosemary, 1 quart	Columbine, 1 cup

Mix together these spices, ground:

Nutmegs, 2   Cloves, ½ cup
Cinnamon sticks, 1 cup

Add and mix:

Orris root, granulated, 1 cup

Toss thoroughly with the leaves and flowers.

Rose Potpourri

Fragrant rose potpourri may be put into small bags or into apothecary jars. For an attractive appearance, press the whole rose geranium leaves against the sides of the jars.

Mix together these dried ingredients:

Rose petals or buds, 1 pound   Pot marjoram blossoms and
Rose geraniums, assorted, 1   leaves, 1 pound
    pound

Mix together:

Rose geranium oil, ½ ounce   Orris root, granulated, ½ pound

Mix all ingredients together. Store in an airtight tin or large, covered stone crock for at least a week.

Herbal Potpourri

This simple potpourri serves as a moth preventive.

Mix together the following dried herbs:

Southernwood (camphor-   Thyme (vulgaris type), 1 cup
    scented), 2 cups   Rosemary, 1 cup
Costmary (*Chrysanthemum
    balsamita*), 2 cups

Rose and Spice Potpourri

After a week of storage in a tight container, this potpourri is ready for packaging in sachet bags made of organdy, calico, net, or lace, or it may be put into glass apothecary jars or small wooden bowls with plastic covers. A few perfect, brilliant-colored petals not added to the mix of spices, which gives a dusty appearance, can be attractively used on the sides and tops of glass jars.

Put into a large bowl the dried petals or buds of:

Roses, 1 quart, or approximately
      1 pound

Add a mixture of:

Cinnamon, cloves, and a little
      nutmeg, ground, 1 cup

Pour onto the mixed petals and spices:

Orris root, granulated, 1 cup   Rose oil, 20 drops

Mix all together thoroughly with the hands. Put the mixture into a tight container and let it mellow for a week.

Herb and Flower Potpourri

This potpourri does not have the strong fragrance of mixtures that include fixatives or oils. However, it has a pleasant garden scent when stirred.

Mix together the following dried flowers:

Rose petals, 2 cups	Oregano flowers, 1 cup
Rosebuds, 1 cup	Marjoram flower heads, 1 cup
Marigold petals, 2 cups	Lavender flowers, 1 cup
Bachelor's button flower heads, 1 cup	

Add the dried leaves of:

Culinary thyme, 1 cup	Lemon verbena, 1 cup
Tarragon, 1 cup	Rosemary, 1 cup
Woodruff, 1 cup	

Hair Rinse

This herbal hair rinse stimulates the scalp and makes the hair shine.

Put in 2 gallons of cool water:

Rosemary leaves, 1 pound

Bring to a boil. Simmer, covered, overnight. Add:

Rosemary oil, 2 drops

Rinse for Blond Hair

Brew in 1 to 4 cups of boiling water for 30 minutes:

Camomile flowers, 1 cup

Strain and cool.

2
Two Culinary Gardens

WE ARE INCLUDING in this chapter two quite different culinary gardens. The first one, which we call the Colorful Garden of Kitchen Herbs, contains 44 herbs that are used in salads, for seasoning, for tea, or as decorations for baked goods. It is also a lovely flower garden that provides us with summer bouquets, material for dried arrangements to cheer us during the winter, and herbs that can be preserved for year-round pleasure.

[41]

The Vegetable and Herb Garden is essentially a useful kitchen garden with salad greens, vegetables for summer menus, and some flowers that double as salad ingredients and as table decorations. Here, too, are flavoring herbs that protect our vegetables from insects and also improve their natural flavor.

A COLORFUL GARDEN
OF KITCHEN HERBS

A walk around this garden of salad and seasoning herbs is a delightful visual and fragrant experience. Almost every plant we brush gives off a pleasant and distinctive aroma. Some, like salad burnet, must be picked to release their good smells—in this case, the wonderfully refreshing scent of freshly cut cucumbers. But the basils, thymes, and mints, especially the orange one, will perfume the air when they have been barely touched. Lemon balm and rosemary are handsome plants with fragrant leaves. They are, of course, necessary in this garden because of their many culinary uses.

The nasturtiums and pot marigolds that we use in salads provide masses of brilliant yellow, orange, and gold flowers in the late summer and fall. Betony, thought by many to have all the best qualities of China tea, has such a long blooming season that it might be grown for its blossoms alone. The spikes of purple flowers are borne on tall stems. The lovely gray-leaved catnip, a treat for the house felines and a source of a tasty tea for people, has attractive gray leaves and dense clusters of pale purple to white flowers through the summer and again in the fall. Hyssop, another tea plant, is also useful in a flower border for its spikes of blue flowers. And the fragrant agrimony holds up its dense spikes of yellow flowers from June until September.

The shape of the beds and the plan of this culinary garden were more or less predetermined by the land on which it was planted. Since several large boulders were in the way of a straight outline, we decided to make a feature of them rather than spend effort in their removal. This gave the garden an irregular pattern that is unified by a broad walk of dark wood chips around the outside. The walk, edged with aged bricks, also provides easy access to the fourteen major beds, and the huge boulders act as seats on which we can rest and enjoy the good smells, the interesting variations in foliage, and the many brilliant and colorful blossoms. The paths within the garden are made of old bricks and are edged with the same material. The raised beds are separated from each other by brick edgings that must be at least two bricks wide.

In the center of the garden is a tall, antique, bronze green weather vane. The large round bed that encircles the vane contains some of our favorite culinary herbs. Angelica is a tall herb with celerylike leaves and spectacular umbels of greenish white flowers. To ensure constant production of its succulent stems and flavorsome leaves for jellies and cake decorations, it is necessary to have several young plants growing around the older ones.

Lovage, too, has celerylike leaves, and they also smell and taste like celery. It is an ancient herb, a favorite in early English gardens and much used by the colonists. Dill, called dill weed, is a tall, single-stalked plant with feathery, light green leaves. The flat clusters of numerous small yellow flowers eventually produce the pungent dill seeds.

The inner circle also includes the beautiful sweet-scented geraniums that make a glorious and fragrant garden by themselves. The various kinds have rose-, fruit-, spice-, and nut-scented leaves that are attractively shaped and often bear interesting markings.

The burnet, tarragon, basils, and parsleys that we cut in quantity for immediate use in salads, seasonings, teas, and cool summer drinks are in the outer beds. Here, too, are chives, Egyptian onions, salad rocket, and chervil that we cut almost constantly during the summer. These "utilitarian" herbs con-

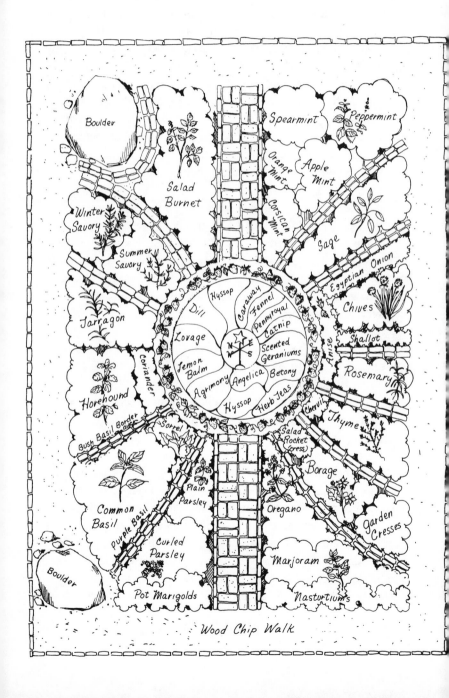

tribute much to this collection of interesting leaf colors and textures, as well as colorful flowers. Picture for a moment the contrast between the reddish purple leaves of the 'Dark Opal' basil and the wrinkled, almost white, leaves of horehound. Then there are the gray and pebbly leaves of common sage crowned by whorls of blue flowers, and the dark green leaves of summer savory that are almost covered by white blossoms in July.

A VEGETABLE AND
HERB GARDEN

When gardeners were made aware of the dangers to people and the environment that are inherent in the use of most pesticides, they began an earnest search for other ways to protect their produce from the ravages of insects and marauders. Both the Herb Society of America and the Bio-Dynamic Association have suggested that many herbs repel insects and in some instances tend to improve the growth and flavor of vegetables when they are planted nearby. Our vegetable and herb garden incorporates many of their suggestions. The combination of vegetables and herbs is a happy one, both for the benefits of companion planting and for the useful and varied harvest it provides.

The edgings of our garden were built out of creosoted wood. This was done partly for clarity of design and partly for ease in dealing with a sloping space that was too wet in spring and too dry in summer. We filled in the framework with garden soil from the rich earth behind our barn and made a plot that has a slight slope for drainage. A retaining wall was built at the low end to keep the soil from seeping away in the torrential rains that hit New England in early fall and spring.

The outer edges of the garden and all the beds are clearly defined in stained wood. The paths are of fine, dark, wood chips. Terra-cotta strawberry jars planted with Fairfax strawberries, a good producing variety, give a decorative character to the garden. A large potted rosemary in the center where the walks join completes the design.

The four center beds are planted with the vegetables that we use most often. One contains white and purple cabbage and kale, all useful for salad and for cooking. For a companion planting we have used dill, which is reputed to improve the growth and health of cabbage. Also in this bed are hyssop and peppermint, that deter the cabbage moth. Another bed is planted with tomatoes. Their companion is basil, both the green and the purple varieties. This herb is a delicious seasoning for tomato dishes and is said to improve the growth and flavor of the fruit. It also repels flies and mosquitoes. A third bed contains eggplant accompanied by tarragon and thyme, which add to the good health of all plants. The fourth bed is planted with peppers and protected by marjoram, which also enhances flavors. The lovage included in this bed improves both the flavor and the health of plants.

Among the outside beds is one of carrots, having sage as its protective companion. The bed of beans contains summer savory, which we trust will deter the bean beetles. Radishes are accompanied by a row of chervil, which should improve their growth and taste. The wormwood outside the lettuce beds is to deter animals.

In another outside protective row we have planted pot marigolds. Camphor-scented southernwood is a tall perennial that has a strong odor unattractive to cabbage moths and all flying pests. We have planted this along another outside row. Here, too, gay nasturtiums double as a protection to squashes and against striped pumpkin beetles. Nasturtiums are a favorite ingredient in tossed salad and add greatly to the color of our garden. Catnip, which discourages the flea beetle, has a place in our outside floral and protective border. Lemon balm is scattered throughout the borders for its fragrant leaves, useful in salads and teas.

Squashes, turnips, beets, and cucumbers and all spreading plants, are grown in a space outside the formal garden. They are bordered on one side by a tall row of handsome tansy, which has a reputation for deterring flying insects, Japanese beetles, squash bugs, and ants. On the other end of these hills of vegetables is a row of borage, a happy companion to squash and beautiful with its bright blue blossoms.

Our combination garden is productive. It is a source of salad greens and small vegetables, a good number of the most used culinary herbs, and enough colorful flowers to decorate tables throughout the season. There are also herbs for vinegars—basil, tarragon, burnet, and dill. There are strawberries for desserts; sage, winter savory, and marjoram for poultry seasoning and stuffings; salad burnet with its cucumber flavor for sandwich fillings and salads; and lemon balm, rosemary, thyme, peppermint, and catnip for teas.

PLANTS FOR THE
CULINARY GARDENS

Agrimony   *Agrimonia eupatoria*

A fragrant plant with numerous small yellow flowers on spikes from June to September. Agrimony has a long history as a healing herb and is still used medicinally in England. Its culinary use is in tea. The whole plant is dried and ground for the hot brew.

Angelica   *Angelica archangelica*
Holy Ghost Plant

Angelica makes a handsome and bold accent or background plant. The clusters of greenish white flowers at the top ends of six-to-seven-foot stems are dramatic. Seeds are a flavoring agent for wines and liqueurs. The French use the candied stems to decorate cakes and buns. The stems are also made into jams and jellies. For jelly, stew stems and leaves in apple juice until all color is removed. Add more juice and more herbs and boil down. Add enough pectin

[47]

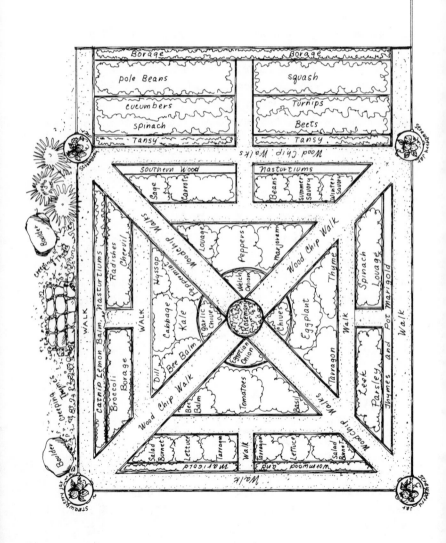

to jell. Pour into a glass and insert a stem or leaf of angelica in each one.

Anise   *Pimpinella anisum*

The feathery gray green foliage and clusters of small white flowers make this a handsome addition to the culinary garden. The seeds are a flavoring for cakes, cookies, candies, applesauce, stews, liqueurs, and wines. Fresh leaves make an interesting salad garnish. We use anise to flavor pork roast. Cover the roast with seeds. Add salt, pepper, garlic, and dry sauterne. Cover and roast.

Bee Balm   *Monarda didyma*

Monarda was made into a hot drink, also called Oswego tea, by American Indians and the colonists. It is an attractive and fragrant plant with excellent white, pink, or red blossoms. The fresh leaves make a tea and flavor apple jelly, fruit salads, and wine cups.

Basil (*Ocimum*)

Basil is a native of India from whence it spread along the Mediterranean to Greece and into Italy. There it was united with the tomato, which had appeared from the New World, and became the seasoning for tomato sauce. It seems to have an affinity for tomatoes.

There are few plants as fragrant as basil. The scent of most can be compared to cloves with a dash of pepper, although some of the bush basils have quite a lemony odor. There are many attractive basils to grow in culinary gardens. Plant them in patterns. Some are little bushy hedges; some have broad leaf rosettes at the top; others have purple, brilliant green, or variegated leaves. Either the fresh or the dried leaves may be used to season salads, vinegars, spaghetti sauces, soups, meats, game, fish, tomato dishes, and pasta.

Bush Basil   *Ocimum basilicum* 'Bush'
The lemony basil or bush basil will grow into a small shrub if it is not crowded. It is a more compact plant and has smaller leaves than sweet basil. All green basils may be used for vinegars. Use a 1-gallon jug of white vinegar. Pour a little off the top and put in enough green leaves to completely fill the jug. Don't be afraid to use too much. A few sprigs of purple ('Dark Opal') basil will color the vinegar pink.

Lettuceleaf Basil   *O. crispum*
This Japanese plant is larger and coarser than sweet basil. The shiny leaves are very much larger, up to three inches in length. We find this the best of the basils for use in salads.

Purple Basil   *O. basilicum* 'Dark Opal'
The reddish purple foliage is quite striking next to green- and gray-leaved plants. It is handsome as a garnish and delicious in salads. We use it to color vinegar.

Sweet Basil   *O. basilicum*
Common Basil
Sweet basil is the most popular of these seasoning herb plants. It has shining, dark green leaves and white to purple flowers. Use as a seasoning for salads, soups, tomato sauce, and spaghetti.

Borage   *Borago officinalis*
This is an interesting plant with rough leaves and lovely blue, pink, or lavender starlike flowers. We like watching it grow better than eating it, but the young leaves impart a cool cucumberlike flavor to salads. Its best use is in punch and other cool drinks.
Marinate borage leaves in a good red wine and add them to

summer punch. Float the little blue blossoms on top. They will make you happy and gay.

Caraway   *Carum carvi*

Caraway is a large and handsome plant with very finely cut leaves and clusters of white flowers in June. Young leaves flavor soups. Seeds are used in sauerkraut, applesauce, apple pie, cookies, cakes, and breads. The oil of the leaves and the seeds are used in kümmel. The root is sometimes eaten as a vegetable; it is similar to parsnips.

Try dipping sliced apples lightly in mayonnaise and sprinkling them generously with caraway seeds.

Catnip   *Nepeta cataria*

A member of the mint family, catnip is a decorative plant with downy leaves and dense spikes of pale purple flowers. Most cats are particularly fond of the dried leaves and flowers, and some people find that a tea made of the leaves is soothing.

Chervil   *Anthriscus cerefolium*

Chervil is an attractive and spreading garden plant with fernlike leaves and clusters of tiny white flowers. It is truly the gourmet's parsley and is important in fine herbs. Use the anise-flavored leaves much as you use parsley—to flavor soups, omelets, salads, sauces, oysters, and as a garnish.

Chive   *Allium schoenoprasum*

The hollow, onion-flavored leaves of chive flavor soups, salads, egg and potato dishes, and hamburger. The plants make attractive borders for culinary gardens, and the lilac, red, and purple flowers are decorative additions to dried arrangements.

Coriander   *Coriandrum sativum*

One of the herb garden's most attractive plants, coriander has lovely lacy foliage and clusters of white and purple flowers. The foliage has a very unpleasant odor, but the seeds, which are used for seasoning and for potpourris, have a sweet smell. The flavorful seeds are used in curry, chopped meat, sausage, stews, gingerbread, cookies, and candy. The foliage is used in Oriental and Mexican cookery.

Early or Belle Isle Cress   *Barbarea verna*
Upland or Winter Cress   *B. vulgaris*

The cresses are salad and seasoning plants of particular value in the early spring. They are sometimes used as substitutes for water cress.

Try a garden cress sandwich. Use homemade bread, sweet butter, and a generous amount of garden cress.

Dill   *Anethum graveolens*

Dill weed is a tall, upright plant with feathery leaves and clusters of yellow flowers that are followed by sharp-tasting dill seeds. Fresh or dried leaves make a good seasoning for fish, salads, green beans, potato salad, beets, vinegars, and soups. Umbels of green dill are used to flavor cucumber pickles.

Make dill butter with dill weed and parsley. Serve it hot over seafood or on boiled potatoes.

Fennel   *Foeniculum vulgare*

Fennel is one of the most ancient herbs. It was first used to improve eyesight and induce weight reduction. Fennel can be used as a tall accent plant. Its bright green, feathery leaves and clusters of yellow flowers make for an interesting contrast with many of the lower-growing culinary herbs. Varieties (*F.v. dulce* and *F.v. piperitum*) are eaten as vegetables. The leaves and stems of *F. vulgare* are used in relishes, salads, and as garnishes. The leaves add flavor to fish sauces, soups, and stews. The seeds flavor puddings, spiced beets, sauerkraut, spaghetti dishes, soups, breads, cakes, candies, and alcoholic beverages.

Garlic   *Allium sativum*

Garlic, too, is an ancient herb. It is said to have been introduced into Europe by the Crusaders and is still included in some Talmudic rituals. Since it is so easily obtainable, herb gardeners may want to include only a symbolic plant or two in the culinary garden. I find the giant garlic (*A. scorodoprasum*) more interesting. Its growth pattern is much like that of the Egyptian onion.

Garlic Chive   *A. tuberosum*

Garlic chive differs considerably from the common chive grown in most gardens. It is taller (two to three feet), has flat scapes, does not have hollow leaves, and bears clusters of white starlike flowers, which are quite fragrant. Use in salads and soups or chopped fine in sandwich mixes.

Geraniums, Rose-scented   *Pelargonium graveolens*

The rose geraniums, which play such a big part in the fragrant and decorative gardens, are also a beautiful and most welcome addition to the culinary herb garden. The leaves are used to flavor sugars, apple jelly, puddings, and tea biscuits.

For tea, use 3 large leaves, 6 cloves, and 2 bags of tea. Brew for 15 minutes. Reduce with hot water as you serve.

Horehound   *Marrubium vulgare*

The wrinkled, almost white leaves of horehound form fascinating rosettes in the early stages of growth. The plants are favorites with flower arrangers. Although horehound may once have had many culinary and medicinal uses, the dried leaves are now almost exclusively devoted to flavoring candy and making a bitter horehound tea.

Hyssop   *Hyssopus officinalis*

The dark, glossy leaves of hyssop are quite boxlike. The plants may be clipped like box, but some should be allowed to develop their pink, blue, or white flowers for garden color. The flavor and

[53]

odor of hyssop does not please all contemporary tastes, so it is included in today's gardens for its historical significance and excellent cutting flowers. There is, however, a new group of people drinking the eighteenth-century teas and reviving interest in hyssop.

Lemon Balm   *Melissa officinalis*
The attractive, crinkled, lemon-scented leaves are crisp and fresh in appearance. The plants make good foliage backgrounds. The dried leaves, which are more flavorsome than fresh ones, make an excellent mild tea and are good for punch, claret cup, fruit desserts, jellied salads, and as garnish for fish.

A lemon balm cooler: Marinate lemon balm leaves in dry white wine. Make coolers with 1 jigger of dry vermouth, a slice of lemon, and the white wine. Pour over ice.

Lovage   *Levisticum officinale*
An ornamental plant from the Mediterranean countries which appeared in many colonial herb gardens. The whole plant smells strongly of celery. The tender leaves add a celerylike flavor to soups, stews, potato salad, green salads, and sauces. The seeds, often included in cordials, may be used to season meat pies, salads, and candies. The leaves do not dry well; they are usually used fresh or frozen.

Marigold   *Tagetes* varieties
The strong-scented leaves of marigolds are said to be the most valuable herbal deterrents to garden pests. They have been found to be especially effective against nematodes and Mexican bean beetles, but are used against other insects as well. The yellow, gold, and orange of their flowers are decorative in the herb garden and also provide table bouquets throughout the summer and fall.

Marjoram   *Majorana hortensis*
Marjoram is one of the most popular garden and culinary herbs. The attractive, velvety, gray green leaves and clusters of white flowers make this a prized plant for the culinary border. It smells

sweet and has a good flavor. Fresh or dried leaves flavor soups, eggs, and vegetables as well as stuffings for pork, lamb, and duck. It is also used in sausage. The English sometimes make a tea of the leaves.

Mint (*Mentha*)

Mints are constantly being harvested from our herb plantings. We cut them in summer for cooling drinks, to make jellies, vinegars, and lamb sauce, and even use the leaves in some of our most refreshing summer bouquets. We also dry mints from June on for teas.

Apple Mint   *Mentha rotundifolia*
This tall gray green mint is prolific. We make at least three harvests of the attractive leaves between June and October and dry them for winter teas.

Orange Mint   *M. citrata*
Bergamot Mint
I find orange mint the most useful of all mints. Both the green and the dried leaves have a wonderful fruity odor and an attractive appearance. Touched with purple in spring, they turn a deep dark green in summer. Use the fresh leaves in punch and fruit salads. The dried leaves make a superb winter tea.

For hot summer days, try an orange-mint drink. Put 1 cup of green mint leaves in boiling water. Add 6 tea bags and allow to steep. Slice oranges in a bowl and add orange mint, orange juice, and lots of ice. Pour the tea into the bowl. Add a jigger of rum to each glass and garnish with a sprig of mint.

Pennyroyal   *M. pulegium*
The aromatic leaves of this creeping plant make an excellent ground cover as well as a good tea. In the eighteenth century it

was used as a flavoring for ground meats. Today it is still used for tea, but is dangerous in large amounts.

Peppermint, English Black   *M. piperita vulgaris*
The dark, reddish purple leaves and bright blossoms and stems of peppermint make it a very decorative plant. It was once a major item of trade between England, America, and Japan, where it has been used in food and medicine for centuries. Dry the leaves for tea and peppermint candy.

For tea, pour boiling water over 1 heaping teaspoonful of leaves for each cup. Steep in a teapot for 10 to 20 minutes.

Spearmint   *M. spicata*
Because of its clean and fresh odor, spearmint was used as a strewing herb in medieval times. Today this green-and-gold-flecked mint is the flavoring agent for iced tea, juleps, jellies, and mint sauces. In the Near East mint is used in salads.

Try making a salad of spearmint, lettuce, and chicory. Serve with a sesame seed dressing.

Nasturtium   *Tropaeolum*
This member of the cress family bears one of the most pleasant herbal flowers. The leaves, seeds, and beautiful yellow and orange flowers are superb for salads and for table decorations. Buds and seeds may be pickled and used like capers.

Onions (*Allium*)

Egyptian Onion   *Allium cepa viviparum*
Top Onion
An attractive back border or accent plant, Egyptian onion rises to three feet and is crowned by a head of new plants. If the seed-

ing tops are not cut, the stems fall to the ground and the bulbs root to start new plants. Young leaves season soups and salads. The strong-flavored bulblets may be pickled or used like mature onions.

Welsh Onion   *A. fistulosum*
Spring Onion

The hollow leaves and flower stalks of the Welsh onion are used for seasoning. The plant bears dense round heads of small white flowers.

Oregano   *Origanum vulgare*

A spreading plant with small pungent leaves and tiny white flowers that grows in knots like marjoram. The fresh or dried leaves of oregano are used to season salads and many tomato dishes, especially tomato sauces. It is also included in fines herbes mixtures.

Parsley, Curly   *Petroselinum crispum*

The bright green leaves of curly parsley make it attractive for the border of culinary gardens if it is planted thickly. Fresh or dried leaves are used in salads, soups, fish sauces, casseroles, omelets, and many vegetable dishes. The Greeks and Romans ate parsley to clear their breath of the odor of garlic and onions and wore crowns of it to banquets to prevent feeling the effects of too much wine.

Parsley, Italian   *P. carum*

Italian parsley has large, flat leaves shaped a little like those of the coarser ferns. Although it is sometimes used as a seasoning, it is usually eaten as a salad green or vegetable.

Spread chopped Italian parsley and slices of mozzarella between layers of parboiled zucchini, sliced tomatoes, and sliced onions. Add ¼ cup of olive oil and top with bread crumbs and Parmesan. Bake at 350° until top is brown.

Pennyroyal. See Mint (page 55).

Pot Marigold   *Calendula officinalis*
These handsome flower garden plants also deserve a special place in the culinary garden. The fresh petals of the beautiful yellow and orange blossoms are a colorful addition to green salads. The dried petals are used to color soups and butters as well as for a tea once considered a cure for internal disturbances.

Rosemary   *Rosmarinus officinalis*
The shining and fragrant leaves make rosemary an ideal plant for a low hedge around an herb bed. There never was enough rosemary. It was mentioned in an Anglo-Saxon herbal of the eleventh century, and its culinary use with salted meats was described in the thirteenth century. Fresh or dried leaves flavor chicken, lamb, soups, stuffings, sauces, jellies, biscuits, and it makes an excellent tea.

Try roast lamb with rosemary. Rub a leg of lamb with garlic salt and place in a roasting pan. Chop rosemary leaves generously over it. Pour in 1 cup of white wine. Cook about 4 hours.

Sage (Blue)   *Salvia officinalis*
Common Sage
Even the name of salvia, meaning to save, suggests its worth. Yet few gardeners grow it for the beauty of its heavy, gray leaves or realize how delightful it is in bloom. Too many treat it as an annual, losing one of its principal advantages—as a permanent border plant or a small shrub after several years of growth. Fresh leaves may be used in cheese sandwiches, soufflés, and stuffings. Dried leaves flavor sausage, cheese biscuits, cheese dishes, pork, poultry stuffings, chicken livers, and are sometimes used for tea.

To make sage biscuits, roll out a baking powder biscuit dough as for a jelly roll. Spread dough with soft butter, cover it with crumbled dried sage, sprinkle with garlic, dried parsley, and grated cheese. Roll up and slice. Bake in moderate oven until lightly browned.

Salad Burnet *Sanguisorba minor*

The evergreen leaves of salad burnet are borne on low and spreading branches that remain on the ground until flowering time. Then the round heads of the deep crimson flowers rise to twelve inches in June. Young, fresh leaves that smell and taste of cucumber may be cut for salads, vinegars, cream cheese, drinks, and green butters. They may also be used as garnishes. The leaves do not dry well.

Make a flavored butter by mixing ½ cup of chopped burnet leaves, ¼ cup of chopped chives, and ¼ pound of sweet butter. Allow the mixture to stand at least overnight until flavors blend. Excellent on homemade bread.

Salad Rocket *Eruca sativa*

Salad rocket is a member of the mustard family that is sometimes grown in the vegetable garden. The large, deeply cut leaves have a strong taste but can be kept delicate by frequent cuttings. They may be chopped up and served in green salads. This plant is used extensively in Italy. It has a strange but fascinating taste.

Savory, Summer *Satureja hortensis*

In summer the bushlike summer savory has narrow, dark green leaves and pale lavender or white flowers with a pink cast. In fall the leaves turn to reddish purple. It is an attractive addition to the culinary garden. Savory has a rather peppery taste that is good when it is used alone or in a mixed blend of herbs. It is an excellent flavoring for all bean dishes and is good in stuffings, rice, soups, gravies, and sauces. Savory dries well when the leaves are green and after they have turned to their exquisite dark red. Then they are so attractive when dried that I use them in winter arrangements.

For an excellent salad, drain and rinse a can of green beans. Add 1 teaspoon of dried shallots and 2 teaspoons of savory. Toss with French dressing.

Savory, Winter   *S. montana*

Winter savory is a low, spreading plant with narrow green leaves and white or blue flowers. A combination of winter savory and basil may be used as a salt substitute. The fresh or dried savory leaves flavor bean dishes, stuffings, rice, soups, and gravies. It is often included in a bouquet garni and can be made into a rather peppery tea.

Shallot   *Allium ascalonicum*

The shallot plant resembles the common onion, but the similarity ends there. The shallot is the most delectable of onions. Cloves of the shallot bulb are used in meat and fish sauces, in vinegars, and in salads.

Sorrel, French   *Rumex scutatus*

No culinary garden should be without this valuable soup and salad herb. The long, shieldlike leaves sometimes have red veins, and the flowers are red brown. Use the leaves for soups, sparingly in salads, for jellies, and in a sauce for beef.

For a quick sorrel soup, fry 2 cups of sorrel leaves in butter until limp. Add 2 cups of chicken broth and cook for 15 minutes. Thicken with cream of chicken soup.

Southernwood   *Artemisia abrotanum camphorata*

The camphor-scented southernwood is a handsome gray shrub with finely divided leaves. It is included in the vegetable and herb garden because the scented leaves are reputed to repel the cabbage moth and other flying pests. It may also be used as a tea.

Strawberry   *Fragaria* varieties

The strawberry jars in the vegetable and herb garden are planted with good bearing varieties. I suggest using 'Baron Solemacher', 'Wood Strawberry', 'Fairfax', or the wild American strawberry *F. virginiana*. Harvest some strawberry leaves for a good medicinal tea.

Tarragon   *Artemisia dracunculus sativa*

This plant was once called little dragon because it was thought to be good for the bites of insects and beasts. It is still effectively used for bee stings. Tarragon is a wonderful seasoning herb. The leaves, with their slight anise flavor, are good for seasoning fish, poultry, steak, vinegars, and salads. It is usually included in fine herb mixtures. Tarragon must be used sparingly, for it has a quite dominating flavor.

To make a seasoning for steak, mix ¼ cup of chopped fresh or dried tarragon leaves and ½ cup of chopped shallot bulbs with ¼ cup of butter. Simmer. Pour over steak.

Thymes   *Thymus vulgaris* 'Broad-leaf English'
                                    T.v. 'Narrow-leaf French'

These are the best culinary thymes. The English one bears an abundance of dark green leaves; the French one is shrubby and woody when old; young plants of French thyme are gray, and the odor is sweeter than that of English thyme. Fresh or dried leaves of thyme add flavor to soups, stuffings, pork, and lamb. It is a strong seasoning that must be used cautiously.

Wormwood   *Artemisia absinthium*

True wormwood is a large shrub with gray leaves. It is a decorative and medicinal plant used in the herb and vegetable garden as a protection against animals. In the house it is a protection against moths and fleas. It was once used in bitters and in the making of absinthe; today it is considered an aphrodisiac and has recently become very popular.

3
A Decorative Garden of Grays and Silvers

FOR YEARS BEFORE designing and planning our gray garden we had collected plants and placed them among greener varieties for contrast. Several good design patterns for the eventual gray and silver garden were discarded, as they did not give us ample room for the astounding number of varieties available. And still we had to consider that we had only scratched the surface of potential residents in a gray garden.

A garden of silvers must be in full sun, for these plants, which come mostly from the arid parts of the world, languish in even slight shade.

In the center of the garden is a cloverleaf knot, outlined in brick and bordered with the classic lavender cotton. Small plants are used, so they may be clipped and trained into place. In the center of the knot is a potted weeping cedrus, which looks better in its clay pot from Italy than it would planted, for the pot raises it and prevents the trailing foliage from sweeping the ground. Inside the border are masses of lamb's ears, which are velvety and almost pure white in the sun. Sun turns foliage of prostrate heath quite silvery.

The beds around the sides of the cloverleaf contain the bulk of the plantings. They are shaped like half-circles and are raised above the walk half a brick high. The walk is made of crushed marble chips, overlaid with fine gray granite to cut down the glare of the marble. The combination of granite and marble is pleasingly soft to the eye. The contrast of the dull brownish red of the bricks is also pleasant with the gray and green leaves.

The many types of plants in the beds are unified by borders of low-growing herbs. Two of the corner beds have borders of gray rosemarys, which must be kept trimmed if they are to remain low. Other corner plantings have silver thyme and variegated ajuga as edgings. The artemisia bed has a border of silver mound, and a bed of nepetas shares its glory with an edging of the gray-leaved June pink and veronica. Gray and spreading snow-in-summer makes a border for the back bed. The front planting is bordered by the beautiful *Sedum seiboldii*, which is a crisp blue to gray. Almost all the plants in this garden are small for ease of placing. The spread of foliage will be tremendous in a year, but a tight planting is more attractive in the early stages of a garden.

Some special additions that must be wintered inside are contained in Italian terra-cotta pots. There is the weeping cedar (cedrus), the *Aloe vera*, and an enormous white licorice plant, too large for any bed, which dominates the back of the garden. Blue spirea is an attractive blue gray shrub, two to three feet in height, which is covered with blue, misty blossoms at the end of August.

Even in the early stages of growth the gray and silver garden has a cool quality reminiscent of moonlight nights or an opalescent sky. Blossoms are shy here; many of the plants like the artemisias have self-color inflorescences. Others, like the nepetas and spirea, produce small blooms of florescent blue. Ajuga and the thymes have white and pale purple blossoms. Dusty miller bears rather insignificant yellow button flowers. Lavender cotton is trimmed before it can flower, and the long candlelike spikes of lamb's ears are removed to keep the plants in scale. Sages are blue at blooming time. Rosemarys produce a few lavender blooms that will be cut to keep the plants trim. All the colors are in low key and restful to the eye.

No gray garden is at its best without a background. We have tried various types of hedges and have settled on silver junipers, since they are in tune with the hoary foliage, and deep green yews for contrast. We like to keep all plants, even the trees, in the herbal category, and the junipers belong here. The berries are used for seasoning and for tea. Boxwood was another possibility for the background, as it has always been associated with herb gardens. In some New England areas it is not completely hardy, but it has grown beautifully for us. We do not cover it in winter, but trim it carefully in spring after the worst of the wind is over. Also in the background are some variegated dogwoods, which were the joy of the garden in the planning stage. Now transplanted beyond the beds, their foliage is in startling contrast to the soft grays and blue greens, and it attracts the eye in a pleasant way.

In this garden are many familiar odors reminiscent of the fragrant herb garden, especially those of the scented geraniums, the lavenders with their sweet foliage and blossoms, rosemarys, and thymes. Nepetas and the sages are pungent, and southernwoods give off pleasing though medicinal scents, reminding us of camphor, lemons, and tangerines. The odors are most noticeable in early morning, at dusk, and at night. Walks through the garden at these times are a special delight.

PLANTS FOR THE
DECORATIVE GARDEN

Acacia   *Acacia baileyana*
Acacia baileyana is a tender mimosalike shrub or small tree with bluish foliage and clusters of yellow flowers. In most of the United States, acacia must be grown in a tub and wintered inside.

Aloe   *Aloe vera*
Aloe vera, sometimes called true aloe and Barbados aloe, is a succulent that is a native of northern Africa. It has a rosette of thick basal leaves with spines. The clusters of orange flowers rise above the one-to-two-foot leaves. In all but the southwestern part of the United States, aloe must be grown in pots and wintered indoors.

Artemisia, Shrubby   *Artemisia aborescens*
Artemisia aborescens is a beautiful plant, relatively new in the United States. A truly silver shrub with finely divided foliage, it makes a striking contrast with flowering and green shrubs.

Artemisia, Fringed   *A. frigida*
The fringed artemisia resembles the more popular 'Silver Mound' in the early part of the growing year, but it grows taller and puts out attractive silver spikes as it matures. It is handsome in bouquets and dries moderately well. The plants may be divided to form a row or low hedge.

Baby's Breath   *Gypsophila paniculata*
The branched panicles of tiny white flowers appear on this bluish green herb in July. The plant is beautiful when in bloom and provides material for many summer bouquets.

Basket-of-Gold *Alyssum saxatile*

Basket-of-gold is a hardy, low-growing plant with foliage that remains gray all season. It bears showers of yellow flowers in spring. The seed cases are translucent and look much like miniature honesty.

Bindweed *Convolvulus cneorum*

A handsome, bushy plant from Greece with gray, lance-shaped leaves and pale pink, morning-glory flowers in summer.

Blue Spirea *Caryopteris incana*

Blue spirea, or bluebeard, is a shrub with gray woolly leaves and violet or lavender blue flowers in the fall. In the North it is better to grow it in a tub and winter it indoors, although it sometimes winters in sheltered spots.

Bugle Weed *Ajuga reptans* 'Variegata'

This creeping bugle weed has green and white leaves and brilliant blue flowers in early summer.

Butterfly Bush *Buddleja crispa*

Butterfly bush is a beautiful flowering shrub. It is a tender perennial that grows to fifteen feet and has long hairy leaves and long panicles of fragrant lilac flowers marked with white.

Carnation *Dianthus caryophyllus*

The carnation, or clove pink, has gray foliage and bears fragrant and handsome rose, pink, or white flowers on stiff stems.

Chrysanthemum *Chrysanthemum ptarmicaeflorum*

This plant looks as though it has been cut out of silver lace. It has heads of small white flowers.

Curry Plant *Helichrysum angustifolium*
Whiteleaf Everlasting

A broad spreading plant, this resembles a large white lavender. It has yellow blossoms, but for the gray and silver garden we think

[67]

it best to keep them cut off. The name describes the odor of the foliage; it is not used in curry.

Dusty Miller   *Senecio leucostachys*
                                                        S. cineraria candissimus

The finely cut leaves of the dusty miller are a necessity in any gray garden. Favorite bedding plants, the leaves of these natives of southern Europe are interesting in flower arrangements and in pressed pictures.

Euryops   *Euryops acraeus*

Euryops is a new and most attractive addition to our garden. It has finely cut, gray foliage and bears numerous yellow flowers in the early spring and summer.

Geranium (*Pelargonium*)

'Gray Lady Plymouth' Geranium
                    Pelargonium graveolens 'Gray Lady Plymouth'

The leaves of Lady Plymouths are cut like those of the rose geraniums, but they have a gray cast with a fine white line edging the leaves.

Nutmeg-scented Geranium   *P. fragrans*

The small, gray green leaves of nutmeg make a marvelous edging for beds of scented geraniums. They conceal the stalks of the taller varieties and unify the outline of the border.

'Old Spice' Geranium   *P.f.* 'Old Spice'

'Old Spice' geranium has a gray, velvetlike leaf with an apple scent. It bears tiny reddish flowers.

Reneforme Geranium   *P. reneforme*

The velvety leaves of the cascading reneforme geranium are small and kidney shaped. It bears minute, purple rose flowers on one-foot stems.

Southernwood-leaved Geranium   *P. abrotanifolium*

The leaves of the southernwood geranium are small and finely feathered with a silvery cast. It bears small white flowers with carmine markings.

Germander   *Teucrium fruticans*

The woolly leaves of this particular germander make it an almost pure white shrub. It bears pale mauve flowers in May.

Heath   *Erica tetralix alba*

When happily exposed to full sun, the leaves of this prostrate heath become silver. It adds an interesting texture to the garden and could be combined with other silver heaths and heathers.

Horehound   *Marrubium vulgare*

The common horehound is hoary and gray, as its name indicates. Young plants are especially attractive because the early growth is particularly wrinkled and woolly. Tips of horehound make wonderful centers for green and gray arrangements. The seed stalks need frequent cutting, for they are filled with rather ugly burrs which do, however, add some charm to dried arrangements. There is a white variety that is not readily available but is worth searching for.

Houseleek, Cobweb   *Sempervivum arachnoideum*

The cobweb houseleek is a beautiful succulent whose leaves form small green or red rosettes. The small pink flowers are borne in clusters. A spider-web system of white threads connects the point of one leaf with the point of another. At times this web can be dense enough almost to cover the leaves.

Ice Plant *Mesembryanthemum crystallinum*
Fig Marigold *Cryophytum crystellinum*
   The prostrate ice plant has fleshy leaves that are covered with shining dots. It bears white or pink flowers close to the leaves.

Jacobinia *Jacobinia suberecta*
   Jacobinia is a tender plant from Mexico and Central America. It must be grown in a tub and wintered indoors in all but the warmest sections of the United States. It bears yellow flowers in long, dense terminal clusters. This plant is sometimes sold as *J. umbrosa*.

Kalanchoe *Kalanchoe fedtschenkoi*
   A native of Madagascar, kalanchoe is a succulent with small, fleshy oval leaves. It has purple flowers in branched terminal clusters.

Lamb's Ears *Stachys olympica lanata*
   The long-stemmed, oblong leaves of lamb's ears are covered with white hairs that give the plant a lovely silvery appearance. The soft and woolly leaves become very white in dry, sunny locations. We do not allow these plants to bloom in a patterned garden, for the spikes spoil the design.

Lavenders (*Lavandula* varieties)

The lavenders are beautiful natives of southern Europe and the Mediterranean countries. They are variations of the "true" lavender known as *L. vera*. The leaves and flowers of most varieties are sweet-scented. The flowers, which grow in spikes or whorls, are blue, lilac, deep violet, purple, pale pink, or white, but the white one is very difficult to find. The foliage is a woolly white or gray.

L. dentata

L. dentata is a tender and decorative plant with deeply cut green or gray leaves. The gray is rare.

L. heterophylla

The spikes of pale blossoms of *L. heterophylla* last throughout most of the summer. The leaves of different shapes are highly scented, but the blossoms have no odor. It makes an excellent greenhouse plant in winter, since it is too tender to be left in the garden.

L. spica

L. spica is a three-to-four-foot shrub with thick and felty, gray leaves. It grows more quickly than *L. vera*, but its tall spikes of flowers are not so fragrant. It is not completely hardy even with cover.

L. stoechas

L. stoechas is a native of the Mediterranean region. Its dark purple flowers are borne in an unusual conelike cluster, and it has hairy leaves. It has little of the characteristic odor of lavender, although it is reputed to have been used in Roman baths. This lavender is only half hardy.

Lavender Cotton   *Santolina chamaecyparissus*
Gray Santolina

The very fine leaves of lavender cotton are blue green at first, but they later turn to a whitish gray. Cut the flower heads from these plants, since they spoil the shape of the plants and are not sufficiently attractive to retain.

Licorice Plant   *Helichrysum petiolatum*
A tropical and shrubby herb with woolly stems and leaves and yellow flowers. The odor is faint and the name misleading. We have a large one in an Italian terra-cotta pot for a center of interest in the back row.

Mint (*Mentha*)

Apple Mint   *Mentha rotundifolia*
The soft, gray green, fuzzy leaves of apple mint permit us to include this fragrant plant in the gray garden. It will take some diligence to keep this rapidly spreading member of the mint family contained in the pattern of the garden. The dwarf English variety can be controlled more easily.

Pineapple Mint   *M.r. variegata*
The white-marked leaves of pineapple mint give the effect of flowers and make a fine garden accent. It is a small form of *rotundifolia*, usually reaching a height of about eighteen inches.

Nepeta, Giant   *Nepeta nuda*
This large relative of catnip is a decorative plant. It has light green, lance-shaped leaves and bears terminal clusters of purple-spotted, white flowers in summer.

Pearly Everlasting   *Anaphalis margaritacea*
Pearly Immortelle
Although a native of the Himalayas, pearly everlasting has naturalized in parts of the United States. The flower heads, which are

very gray and stiff, are often dried for arrangements. We find them a necessity for our wreaths.

Pink, Cheddar *Dianthus gratianopolitanus*
The familiar, low-growing pink makes an excellent border plant. It has gray, almost white, foliage and small pink blossoms in June. Cheddar pink grows tight to the ground and remains gray.

Pussy Toes *Antennaria aprica*
The hairy leaves of the creeping pussy toes make a silver carpet in the garden. Its small pink flowers may be dried for arrangements.

Rosemary *Rosmarinus officinalis*
(Gray-leaved variety)
This is a rapid grower with broad, soft leaves that are unlike the dark and glossy needles of the blue-flowered rosemary. The gray-leaved rosemary is best when kept clipped for hedges.

Rosemary, Prostrate *R. officinatis prostratus*
R. lavendulaceus
The prostrate rosemary has the same marvelously scented leaves and blue flowers of the upright plant, but it has a spreading habit. It is distinct from *R. humilis*, which is most often used in rock gardens in warm climates.

Rue *Ruta graveolens*
The divided and notched, blue green leaves of rue are a valuable addition to the texture and color of the garden. Its yellow flowers are followed by red brown seedpods that may be used in dried arrangements. Always plant rue away from paths so that it will not be brushed as visitors walk by. At times it causes skin irritations.

Sage (*Salvia*)

Clary Sage   *Salvia sclarea*
Clear Eyes

This famous old medicinal sage, called Clear Eyes, is certainly one of the most beautiful herbs in the garden. The rosettes of hoary leaves are blue gray and catch the dew in the morning, so they always seem to shimmer. The blossoms are magnificent heads of a mixture of white, blue, and pink, varying as the blossoms age and as bracts are formed. The rare combination of blooms and colored bracts remains on three-foot stems for at least a month. After this it dies, sending out hundreds of seeds that must be allowed to grow or this beautiful biennial will be lost.

Dwarf Sage   *S. officinalis* variety

There is a dwarf variety of officinalis. It smells like the common garden sage varieties, and its leaves are as gray, thick, and fuzzy, but they are narrower and the plant stays small.

Purple Sage   *S.o. purpurescens*

The dark purplish leaves and deep purple stems of purpurescens make it one of the most decorative of all the sages. Since it is not hardy, it must be sacrificed or wintered inside.

Russian Sage   *Perovskia atriplicifolia*

The leaves and stems of the wide and bushy Russian sage have a gray green appearance because they are covered with a kind of hairy down. The plant bears long clusters of violet blue flowers in late summer.

Silver Sage   *Salvia argentea*

The whitest of the gray sages. The large woolly leaves make snowy mounds in the early part of its very slow growth. It is best to cut off the tall growth so the garden pattern is not distorted. Silver sage must be grown in well-drained, sunny land.

Variegated Sage   *S. officinalis* 'Tricolor'
A variety of common sage that has gray green leaves with yellowish and pink veins. The leaves turn a soft red. Variegated sage must be wintered inside in colder climates.

Samphire   *Crithmum maritimum*
This fleshy, pungent herb has glaucous leaves shaped like small hands. It bears very small white or yellowish flowers. In England where it was once used for pickling, it grew just above the waterline on the Cliffs of Dover. It finds its way into the decorative garden because of its blue gray foliage.

Sedum

Sedum dasyphyllum
A low, gray green plant that bears clusters of pink flowers in summer.

S. glaucum
S. hispanicum 'Bithynicum'
Sedum glaucum is a gray plant that is often used for carpet bedding.

S. sieboldii
The glaucous foliage of *Sedum sieboldii* sometimes has pinkish edges, giving the plant a bluish gray effect. It has rosy purple flowers in the fall. Sieboldii is a superb edging plant.

S. spathulifolium
The fleshy, gray green leaves of this sedum make a cushionlike plant. In spring it bears clusters of bright yellow flowers. *S.s. pur-*

pureum has purple leaves that are covered by a gray waxlike coating. It does not flower well.

Sheep's Fescue
Blue Fescue

Festuca ovina glauca

This glaucous, tufted grass makes an excellent border plant. It has a modern look about it.

'Silver King' Artemisia

Artemisia albula 'Silver King'

A. albula, a stunning accent or background plant, is very white. 'Silver King' creates an almost cloudlike effect in the garden and is indispensable for arrangements of fresh and dried flowers.

'Silver Mound' Artemisia

A. schmidtiana nana 'Silver Mound'

'Silver Mound' is feathery and elegant at all stages of growth. It must be cut back in late August to be at its silvery best in September and October.

Snow-in-summer

Cerastium tomentosum

Snow-in-summer is one of the grayest and most persistent of the low-growing and spreading plants. The lovely silver foliage must be cut back after the white blooms have gone.

Southernwood

Artemisia abrotanum

Southernwood is among the most attractive shrubs for the herb garden. We grow the lemon- and the camphor-scented kinds. They both have a greenish gray cast, although not truly gray.

Tansy, Silver

Tanacetum densum amanum

Silver tansy is low-growing with gray, finely cut leaves. A lovely ground cover, native of Turkey, and very rare.

Thyme

Creeping Thyme   *Thymus serpyllum* varieties

The creeping thymes that are gray and woolly include the close-growing, fine-leaved lanuginosus, which is almost white in dry ground, the *britanicus*, which has longer stems but is very gray, and Hall's woolly thyme, which has grayish, hairy leaves and bears pink blossoms in early spring.

French Thyme   *T. vulgaris* 'Narrow-leaf French'

This is one of the common thymes usually grown in culinary gardens. Its growth pattern is, however, so attractive and it is so fragrant that it is a charming addition to any formal garden. The leaves are very gray. Its growth is so rapid that a tiny plant hardly visible at planting time expands into a low shrub by late summer.

Silver Thyme   *T. serpyllum argenteus*

Silver thyme has a variegated leaf that becomes more silvery as it grows to a small shrub.

Veronica   *Veronica incana*

Veronica incana is a downy white or gray plant with narrow leaves that bears spikes of pink or blue flowers in June. A native of Russia and northern Asia.

Weeping Cedar (Cedrus)   *Cedrus atlantica* 'Blue Atlas'

Most atlas cedars have bluish green, needlelike leaves, although some forms have silver leaves and drooping branches. They grow to considerable heights in their natural habitats, but a tub helps restrict the growth.

Wormwood

Wormwood   *Artemisia absinthium*
Wormwood is a gray, shrublike herb that makes a decorative background plant. The English have a silver variety that is not quite so tall but is more spreading. It is sometimes available under the name *A.a.* 'Lambrook Silver'.

Cudweed Wormwood   *A. purshiana*
Cudweed wormwood is much like 'Silver King,' but it has a thicker and broader leaf. It adds an excellent gray note to the border of the garden and to dried bouquets.

Roman Wormwood   *A. pontica*
The fine gray foliage of Roman wormwood is lacy and decorative on the plant and in bouquets. It seldom blooms.

Yarrow   *Achillea* 'Moonshine'
This yarrow has handsome and silvery foliage that is finely cut. It bears large heads of pale yellow flowers from June until September. The flowers are marvelous material for dried arrangements.

Yarrow, Creeping   *A. tomentosa*
Creeping yarrow is a woolly, mat-forming plant with leaves that resemble a creeping starfish. It bears small, but numerous, yellow flowers in June. They dry well for winter bouquets.

Gardens
Through
History

4

A Shakespearean Garden

YOU MAY MEET Shakespeare in your own garden. His works speak not only of the Elizabethan gardens of the great European families of the sixteenth and seventeenth centuries, which he used as settings in plays like *Romeo and Juliet*, but also of many other types. There is the simple dooryard garden that he passed through in visiting Anne Hathaway's cottage. He also described the wild

[81]

"gardens" of the fields and meadows and the medicinal plants growing outside the castle walls where Friar Lawrence collected potent herbs to induce Juliet's sleep.

Kitchen gardens flourished in Shakespeare's time (1564–1616) and were sometimes combined in grandiose garden plans. They were a part of the thirty acres of planting suggested by his contemporary, Francis Bacon (1561–1626), as the ideal garden and were actually developed on several of the large estates. Many of the smaller manors combined the orchard and the kitchen garden, as had been done in the monastery enclosures.

Some of the ancient manor houses and medieval village homes used the "close" and the "pleasance," a type of planting that was intimate and almost a part of the house. Here, one stepped into a small garden surrounded by walls, sometimes of stone, often of brick, but definitely enclosed, with a gate at the entrance. Every means was used to engender privacy. It was an outdoor living room, truly a place for repose and meditation. Since conserving space was important in this small confine, a part of the orchard became attached to the walls. Espaliered trees were both decorative and practical. Grapes spanned the walls or were carefully trimmed into a producing arbor; herbs, flowers, and fruits and vegetables all grew in this enchanted area.

Emphasis was placed on fragrant plants as well as on some that were medicinal. Herbs for strewing the cold stone floors were important from medieval times until about 1800, and sweet-smelling snippings were treasured for this household use. The stillroom, a working part of every medieval household, produced essences and medicines. Here, usually separated from the main building, the sweet herbs were distilled, washing waters made, aromatic perfumes produced, and medicines that would combat the ills of winter were compounded. Scents were especially important because of the poor sanitation and because it was the belief of the physicians from monastic times on into the scientific age that just to draw in sweet essences from living flowers was of great benefit to physical well-being. Perhaps it is.

PLAN OF THE
ELIZABETHAN GARDEN

The Elizabethan garden, which was an adaptation of the patterned gardens of the East, was balanced in design and adjoined the Tudor house. It was frequently bordered or hedged with paths carefully planned to implement the pattern and to bring the visitor near the plants. Flower beds in the form of knots were edged with box, thrift, thyme, santolinas, and hyssop. The outer hedge, which was composed of fragrant green material, enclosed this place of quiet and repose and gave privacy and a mysterious air to the garden. Here hedge roses such as eglantine and other flowering varieties of the rose mingled with privet and hawthorn. The latter was often trimmed and trained by bending down branches so they would reroot into what was known as the quick-set hedge. This, with the sharp spines of the eglantine, or sweet briar, made an impenetrable wall that kept out dogs, cattle, and all marauders.

The plantings in the larger gardens were approached from a terrace or a succession of different levels that afforded a view of the whole pattern.

THE "CURIOUS
KNOTTED GARDEN"

This favorite form of the Elizabethan garden came into use in England about 1525. Although it was new to the Tudor gardeners, it was a very popular form of the East Indian gardens of luxury, where the Moguls took their pleasure and dreamed away the hours. The English adapted this Eastern form to the contours of their houses and lands, and they made the knots of plants that would survive the colder climate. The geometric forms were kept, but planting became thicker, and flowers were massed and blended

[83]

together inside the knots, sometimes in rainbow shadings. The various heights were well considered, and those that grew well together were so planted. A vast number of flowers were known at this time, and the great pleasances of the rich, the cottage plantings of the poor and the middle class, bloomed alike, as described by Gervase Markham (1568–1637) in *The Countrie Farm*:

> The Garden of Pleasure shall be set about and compassed with arbors made of Jessamin, rosemarie, box, juniper, cypress-tree, savin, cedars, rose trees, and other dainties first planted and pruned according as the nature of every one doth require, but after brought into some form and order with willow or juniper poles, such as may serve for the making of arbors. The ways and alleys must be covered and sown with fine sand, well beat, or with the powder or the sawing of marble, or else paved handsomely with good pit stone. This garden, by means of a large path of the breadth of six feet, shall be divided into two equal parts; the one shall contain the herbs and flowers to make nosegays and garlands, as March violets, Provence gillyflowers, Indian gillyflowers, marigolds, lily connally [lily of the valley], daffodils, Canterbury bells, purple velvet flowers, anemones, cornflag, mugwort, lilies, and other such-like; and it may indeed be the Nosegay Garden. The other part shall have all the sweet smelling herbs whether they be such as bear no flowers, or, if they bear any, yet they are not put into nosegays alone, but the whole herb be with them such as Southernwood, wormwood, pellitory, rose-marie, jessamine, marierom [marjoram], balm-mints, pen-nyroyal, cost marie, hyssop, lavender, basil, sage, savory, rue, tansy, thyme, camomile, mugwort, bastard marierom [oregano], nept, sweet balm, all good, anis, horehound, and others such-like; and this may be called the garden for herbs and good smell. These sweet herbs and flowers for nosegays shall be set in order upon beds and quarters of such-like length and breadth as those of the kitchen gar-

den. Others in mazes made for the pleasing and recreating of the sight, and other some are set in proportions made of beds interlaced and drawn one within another or broken off with borders, or without borders.

Our knot borders today are largely formed of santolinas, since this is an herb that takes cutting kindly, is easy to control, grows reasonably fast, and makes an interesting line of gray or green.

For these knots, John Parkinson, a seventeenth-century writer on plants, suggests thrift, hyssop, and germander, but his enthusiasm for box is boundless, and rightly so for climates no more severe than that of England. In New England's uncertain temperatures we have witnessed too many disastrous results of winter's rigors to recommend box except with warning. Parkinson recommends: "Chiefly above all herbs the small low, or dwarf French or Dutch box, because it is evergreen, thick, and easily cut and formed."

Parkinson also mentions many outlandish flowers to be found in the English gardens of the Tudors, chief of which was the "greate Nonsuch Daffodil or Incomparable Daffodil—the cup doth very well resemble the chalice that in former dayes with us and beyond the Seas is still used to hold the sacramental wine, that is, with a narrowed bottome and a wide mouth."

FLOWERS OF SHAKESPEARE

Canon Ellacombe, vicar of Britton, in Gloucestershire, wrote, the most complete book about plants of Shakespeare in 1878, and quotations from his introductory remarks are well worth repeating. Since the introduction is long, we must eliminate many fine passages, though regretfully. He begins:

A lover of flowers and gardening myself, I claim Shakespeare as equally a lover of flowers and gardening. He exhibits a very fair though not perhaps a very deep knowledge of plants. I do not believe that he was ever a professed gardener and I am quite sure that he can in no sense be claimed as a brother botanist in the scientific sense of the term. His knowledge of plants was simply the knowledge that every man may have who goes through the world with his eyes open to the many beauties of Nature that surround him, who tries to find out something of the inner meaning of the beauties he sees, and to carry with him some of the lessons that they have doubtless meant to teach. He had the great gift of being able to describe what he saw in a way that few others have ever arrived at. It was not by long descriptions, but by a few simple words, a few natural touches, and a few well-chosen epithets, which bring the plants to us in the freshest and often most touching way.

Canon Ellacombe comments on the "thoroughly English character" of Shakespeare's descriptions. Wherever the scenes are laid, the characters continue to be Englishmen of his day. This is certainly true of the plants and the flowers we meet within the plays; they are thoroughly English plants that, with a few exceptions, he saw in the hedgerows and woods of Warwickshire or in his own or his friends' gardens. The descriptions are fresh and real; they tell of the country and the outdoor life he loved, and they never "smell of the study lamp." The canon comments in detail on the contemporaries of Shakespeare who spoke of plants in classical allusions, naming them "because it was the right thing for a classical scholar to do." Two great exceptions to this rule were Ben Jonson (1573?–1637) and William Browne (1591?–1645?). Geoffrey Chaucer (c. 1340–1400) before Shakespeare's time and Robert Herrick (1591–1674) after him drew their plants and the descriptions of them from life, and sang of them as they saw them.

Shakespeare introduces flowers only in their right places. The number of flowers mentioned and introduced is large, but the number he omits, and which he must have known, is also very large, and well worth noting. Many common and lovely flowers are not presented, such as the foxglove, snowdrop, and lily of the valley;

because when he names a plant or flower, he does so not to show his own knowledge, but because the particular flower or plant is wanted in the particular place in which he uses it. The range of his observation is very broad. He gathers plants from many places, "the turfy mountains," the "flat meads," the "bosky acres," and the "unshrubbed down."

Our Shakespeare garden is a small version of Elizabethan gardens. It includes plants popular in Shakespeare's day, and about which he wrote. There are many others, so each lover of the poet and gardens can create something of his or her own.

THE CAPRILANDS
SHAKESPEARE GARDEN

It has long been my desire to produce a garden in which all the herbs of the great poet's day were grown and marked with appropriate quotations. The structure of this planting presented many difficulties. Backgrounds and enclosures, which require years to grow or much labor to produce, were our chief concern. High walls in the space that was available were impossible, and it seemed best to use the materials at hand to unify these garden importations from foreign soil, in order to make it a part of New England. Fortunately, many Shakespeare flowers are also New England flowers, for our early colonists brought to the New World not only Tudor architecture in a simple form, but also the plants and the attendant lore and uses of their home gardens. Mediterranean herbs had become English and were a part of the memories of the homeland. Thus, an herb garden actually containing plants originally from all parts of the earth will seem appropriate in England and New England. Few will think of lavender as anything but a native English plant, for it thrives in England probably better than in any other spot in the world; but its home is actually in France and the Canary Islands. Rosemary, bay, savory, basil, calendula, the Mary buds, even many of the thymes, all so much a part of the English scene, were once imports from the warm shores of the Mediterranean.

Low walls surround our garden to give the sense of enclosure. The background is an old stone wall that held back the cattle in the days when Caprilands was a working farm. The walls are made of two double rows of fieldstone with a generous filling of good growing soil between them. They surround the garden area and are here planted with lavender, winter savory, ivy, samphire, thyme, and box. Succulents, especially samphire, thrive in great abundance, creeping over the stones, at times covering them with gray leaves and occasional blossoms. The inside space is divided into two levels. The entrance is two simple steps planted with thyme. Although our garden is open at both ends, one could be closed, with a sun dial for a focal point.

At the corners of the walls, tall rosemary shrubs sweep over the edge. Just outside the garden foxgloves, companulas, fennel, larkspurs, and delphiniums find shelter for their great height in the stone wall. We have combined both herbs and flowers, secure in the knowledge that if we wish to call this an herb garden, we may do so with impunity, since these flowers are mainly those of herbal uses.

Shakespearean quotations are lettered on slate, since that color goes so well with old walls. To insure permanency, the quotations are in white house paint which lasts through several seasons.

The garden plan shows the simple primitive pattern of our garden, which is worked out with old chestnut two-by-fours and has small benches made of the same ancient material. The paths are covered with finely crushed granite grits. A hedge of roses is planted just outside one of the stone walls.

Unfortunately, our list of plants for the Shakespeare garden, like Canon Ellacombe's, does not give every plant reference and "pick each flower and note each plant which he [Shakespeare] has felt worthy of notice." From that very long list we have selected those plants available today and easily grown by the average gardener.

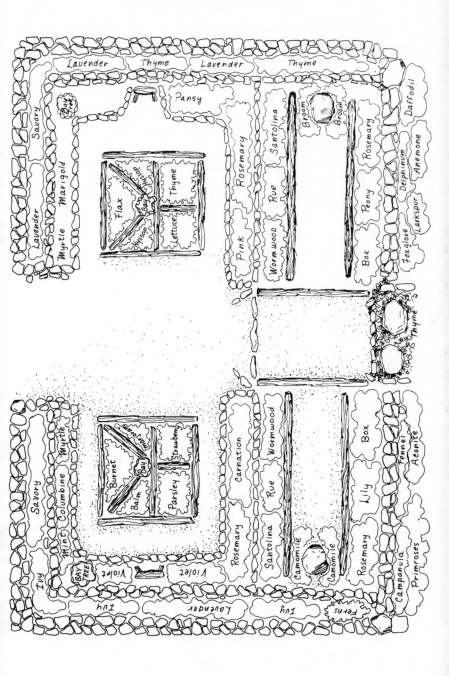

HERBAL PLANT QUOTATIONS
FROM SHAKESPEARE

Balm   *Melissa officinalis*

> *The several chairs of order, look you,*
> *   scour*
> *With juice of Balm and every precious*
> *flower.*
>
> MERRY WIVES OF WINDSOR

> *As sweet as Balm, as soft as air,*
> *   as gently.*
>
> ANTONY AND CLEOPATRA

Many references in the plays pertain to a balsam imported from
the East and called balm. These refer to *melissa*, or lemon balm,
an attractive foliage plant with lemon-scented leaves.

Bay Tree   *Laurus nobilis*

> *'Tis thought the King is dead. He*
> *   will not stay*
> *The Bay trees in our country are*
> *   all withered.*
>
> RICHARD II

> *Enter, solemnly tripping one after*
> *   another, six personages clad*
> *   in white robes, wearing on their*
> *   heads garlands of Bays or Palms*
> *   in their hands.*
>
> HENRY VIII

This is the seasoning bay, a native of the Mediterranean countries. It is a beautiful shrub or tree with fragrant, glossy, dark

green leaves. In our climate it must be grown in pots or transferred to them for the winter.

Box   *Buxus*

> *Get ye all three into the Box-tree.*
> TWELFTH NIGHT

Although Shakespeare mentions the box tree only once, it is well known that this tree played a major part in the gardens of his day. The deep green of the tree made it a symbol of Pluto, the god of the world of the dead. The presence of box in English gardens is thought to be attributable to the Romans, who used it lavishly in their transplanted gardens. In England box found a happy climate and became a part of the framework on which the Tudor gardens were built. It is as ancient as the Old Testament. It was the plant of necromancers. To dream of box signified a happy marriage, prosperity, and longevity. Box decorated the Tudor house from Candlemas Day until Easter.

Broom   *Cytisus scoparius*

> *I'm sent with Broom before*
> *To sweep the dust behind the door.*
> MIDSUMMER NIGHT'S DREAM

This beautiful and usually hardy shrub blooms with fragrant yellow or white flowers, and its trailing growth is decorative throughout the year. Under its Latin name of *Planta genista*, it gave its name to the Plantagenet family, in the time of Henry II. It was the special flower of the Scotch, but also highly esteemed on the Continent.

Burnet   *Sanguisorba minor*

> *The even mead that erst brought forth*
> *The freckled Cowslip, Burnet, and Sweet Clover.*
> HENRY V

Burnet, a salad herb, was used in parts of England as a forage crop for cattle, so its inclusion here with other meadow plants is understandable. It has since become well known for its cucumber flavor and is a culinary nicety.

Camomile, Roman   *Anthemis nobilis*

> *Though the Camomile the more it is*
> *trodden on the faster it grows,*
> *yet youth, the more it is*
> *wasted the sooner it wears.*
>
>   HENRY IV

The garden emblem of sweetness and humility, camomile is often called the apple of the earth. It has fine bright green foliage, and a smell of apples when walked upon. The flowers look like tiny daisies.

Carnation   *Dianthus caryophyllus*

> *Carnations and streaked gillyflowers,*
> *the fairest flowers of the season.*
>
>   WINTER'S TALE

Carnations once were called coronations because the flowers were used to make wreaths, crowns, and garlands. The name *dianthus*, under which most pinks parade today, meant flower of Jove. Chaucer called it the clove gilliflower, and from its use in wine bowls it was called sops in wine. The name *caryophyllus*, or nut leaves, came from the old name of the Indian clove tree. It was transferred to the carnation because the flower was so strongly scented of cloves. It is thought to have traveled from Normandy with William the Conquerer.

Columbine   *Aquilegia vulgaris*

> *There's fennel for you and columbines.*
>
>   HAMLET

A Shakespearean Garden

I am that flower,
That mint, that columbine!
LOVE'S LABOUR'S LOST

Called the dove plant, columbine was also thought to be the favorite plant of lions and thus was known also as *Herba leonis.* It was highly regarded for its medicinal values. English wild columbines are often found in deep purple and blue. In religious symbolism, the columbine signified the seven gifts of the Holy Spirit. Little doves were formed by the five petals of the flower. Early Flemish painters changed the five petals to seven to make the flower agree with the teaching of the church.

Flax

Linum grandiflorum
L. perenne
L. trigynum
L. usitatissimum

Excellent, it hangs like Flax in
a distaff.
TWELFTH NIGHT

Go thou; I'll fetch some Flax and
white of eggs
To apply to his bleeding face.
KING LEAR

My wife deserves a name
As rank as any Flax-wench.
WINTER'S TALE

Flax, one of the great items of commerce in past ages, was a native of Egypt and was mentioned in the Book of Exodus. It was carried by traders all through the civilized world and was easily naturalized in the mild and moist climate of England. It was a most useful herb, and produced linen, linseed oil, linseed meal, cake, and flax seed for poultices. Flax legends are many. Great virtues were attributed to it, and it figured largely in spring and mid-summer festivals. All the many linums are beautiful in the garden.

Hyssop *Hyssopus officinalis*

> *'Tis in ourselves that we are thus or*
> *thus. Our bodies are gardens;*
> *to which our wills are gardeners; so*
> *that if we will plant nettles or sow*
> *Lettuce, set Hyssop or weed up Thyme;*
> *supply it with one gender of herbs or*
> *distract it with many, either to have*
> *it sterile with idleness or manured*
> *with industry; why the power and*
> *corrigible authority of this lies*
> *in our wills.*
>
> OTHELLO

Hyssop is a handsome, hardy, and rather woody shrub with shining leaves that are narrow and pointed. It has bright blue, white, or pink blossoms.

Iris *Iris*

> *Awake, awake, English nobility!*
> *Let not sloth dim your honors new begot:*
> *Cropped are the flower-de-luces in your*
> *   arms;*
> *Of England's coat one half is cut away.*
>
> KING HENRY VI

The iris, once classed among the lilies and so mentioned in Shakespeare, is our "flower-de-luces." In Egypt the iris was the symbol of eloquence and power and adorned the brow of the sphinx. The petals of the flower, of which there are three, decorated the scepter of the early monarchs of Egypt, Babylon, and Greece and represented faith, wisdom, and valor. Lovely Iris, a messenger of the Gods, gave her name to the many-colored flowers as prismatic as the rainbow, the bridge upon which she descended to earth.

Iris became the flower of France in the time of Clovis. Saint Clotilde had a vision of the flower, a good omen, which caused Clovis, her husband, to remove the frogs from his shield to substitute the iris. Louis VII also dreamed of the iris, and in 1137 it became his heraldic device. It was known as the fleur de Louis, from which came the name *fleur-de-lis*.

Ivy, English   *Hedera helix baltica*

> *Sleep thou, and I will wind thee in*
> *my arms, the female ivy so*
> *Enrings the barky fingers of the*
> *elm.*

MIDSUMMER NIGHT'S DREAM

For the Shakespeare garden English ivy seems most appropriate. It grows well, is green winter and summer, and spreads over the low stone walls.

Lavender   *Lavandula vera*

> *Here's flowers for you,*
> *Hot Lavender, sweet Mints, Savory,*
> *Marjoram.*

WINTER'S TALE

Although lavender and its varieties are among the most important plants in the herb garden, it is mentioned only once by Shakespeare. This is probably because its introduction into England was relatively recent and it was not at that time so commonly identified with English gardens. A native of the dry barren places in the mountains of southern France, and farther south in the Canary Islands, it found its happiest home in England.

Lettuce   *Latuca sativa*

> *If we will plant nettles or sow*
> *lettuce*
>   OTHELLO

This herbal vegetable came to England with the Romans and was largely cultivated by the Anglo-Saxons, who understood its narcotic properties for inducing sleep. Because it was pleasant-tasting and soothing, it was given the name of sleepwort.

Lily, Crown Imperial   *Lilium*

> *Lilies of all kinds . . .*
>   WINTER'S TALE

From Parkinson we gather that a great variety of lilies were known to the Elizabethan gardeners. First in popularity was *L. candidum*, the pure white stately lily. The tiger and martagon, or Turk's-cap, were also popular. The crown imperial, or *Fritillaria imperialis* of the lily family, was next in favor to the white lily; a native of Kashmir, it was taken to Constantinople and into Vienna from whence it came to England.

Marigold   *Calendula officinalis*

> *The Marigold which goes to bed with*
> *the sun*
> *And with him rises, weeping.*
>   WINTER'S TALE

> *Hark, hark, the lark at heaven's gate*
> *sings,*
> *And Poebus 'gins arise,*
> *His steeds to water at those springs*
> *On chaliced flowers that lies;*
> *And winking Mary-buds begin to ope*
> *their golden eyes;*

> *With everything that pretty is—My lady,*
>   *sweet, arise:*
>   *Arise, arise.*

CYMBELINE

Marigold, our calendula, has had many names through the centuries, for it was one of the most loved of wild and garden flowers. An early name is *Spousa solis*, the spouse of the sun, "because it sleeps and is wakened with him." An old English name is ruddess; another, gold flower. Chaucer calls it "yellow Goldes." Medieval monks placed it in their Mary gardens and added the name of Mary to the descriptive gold. According to legend, Mary wore this flower, the "Mary-buds" of Shakespeare, in her bosom, preferring it to all others. The term *calenda* was derived from the fact that in its warm Italian home it bloomed on the first day of every month. It was also the flower for Lady Day, March 25.

Other names of marigold are Sun's Bride, Husbandman's Dial, Sun's Herb. It was called *Heliotropesolsequieum* by the Greeks, who believed that its origin was with the nymph Clytie, who gazed all day at the sun in hopeless adoration and was at last transformed into a flower that lived only for the kiss of the god of the heavens. The marigold was sometimes called souvenir, since in the time of Henry VIII, court ladies often wore wreaths of "goldes" mixed with heart's ease. The marigold was the favorite flower of Margaret of Orleans. From Provence comes the name *gauche-fer*, which compares to the shining gold disk of the flower to the polished shield worn on the left arm of a warrior.

A dream of marigolds was a happy one, for it foretold prosperity, riches, success, wealth, and a happy marriage.

One story concerns four wood nymphs, attendants of Diana. They were all in love with the handsome Apollo, and their quarreling so displeased the goddess that she turned them into marigolds. In this guise they gazed forever on their idol. They would "ope their golden eyes" in the morning with "his light" and go "to bed with the sun" at night. They became a symbol of jealousy and a warning to all maids to avoid this sin.

Marjoram
Majorana hortensis (sweet)
Origanum vulgare (wild)

The Lily, I condemned for your hand,
And buds of Marjoram had stolen
thy hair.

SONNET 99

Indeed, sir, she was the sweet
Marjoram of the Salad, or rather
the Herb-of-grace.
ALL'S WELL THAT ENDS WELL

Marjoram is a favorite annual that comes easily from seed. In Elizabethan times, several of the origanums were grown, and several of these are now called oregano.

Mint (English Black Peppermint)
Mentha piperita vulgaris

I am that flower,
That Mint,
That Columbine.
LOVE'S LABOUR'S LOST

Mints are an important part of every herb garden, large or small. They are of ancient origin and were used to perfume the air, to season foods, and to clear the head. They were thought to produce wisdom in the very breathing in of their scent. In Shakespeare's time, mints were gathered from the wild as they were in early America. They were also appreciated for their contribution to the fragrance of a garden walk.

Myrtle
Myrtus communis
M.c. microphylla

Venus with young Adonis sitting
by her Under a Myrtle shade
began to woo him.
PASSIONATE PILGRIM

Then sad she hasted to a Myrtle grove.
VENUS AND ADONIS

Venus and her nymphs were protected from the advances of the satyrs while they were bathing. The myrtle tree folded around the goddess and concealed her. From this incident, myrtle, the plant of love, was dedicated to Venus and became a favorite in the English garden. It was often grown in tubs so it might be moved easily to decorate terraces or indoor plantings. It is half-hardy, and in a sheltered English garden might winter outside.

Pansy *Viola tricolor*

Pansies—that's for thoughts.
HAMLET

*The little Western flower upon which
the bolt of Cupid fell.*
MIDSUMMER NIGHT'S DREAM

The pansy of this time was the little *Viola tricolor*, known to us as Johnny-jump-up, or heartsease. The larger, more colorful pansy of our day was not developed until 1875. This small flower was magical, as readers of *Midsummer Night's Dream* will remember; for the juice squeezed upon Titania's eyelids and upon the others asleep in the forest caused much interesting confusion. The viola was also deemed to be medicinal, especially as a heart medicine.

Parsley *Petroselinum crispum*

*I knew a wench married in the afternoon
as she went to the garden for Parsley
to stuff a rabbit.*
TAMING OF A SHREW

Peony   *Paeonia albiflora*

> *Thy banks with Pionied and Lilied brims,*
> *Which spongy April at thy hest betrims*
> *To make cold nymphs chaste crowns.*
>
>   TEMPEST

The peonies Shakespeare wrote of are very popular spring-blooming perennials in American gardens. The solitary and dense flowers of many colors sometimes measure six inches across.

Pink   *Dianthus gratianopolitanus*
                                                         D. plumarius

> *This pink is one of Cupid's carriers;*
> *Clap on more sail—pursue!*
>
>   MERRY WIVES OF WINDSOR

Cheddar pink, *D. gratianopolitanus*, has almost white foliage and small but dense pink blossoms with a spicy scent in June. It stays close to the ground and so makes an excellent border plant.

D. plumarius is another mat-forming plant with gray foliage. Its fragrant flowers vary from rose to white.

Rose   *Rosa* varieties and species

> *So sweet a kiss the golden sun*
>   *gives not*
> *To those fresh morning drops upon*
>   *the rose.*
>
>   LOVE'S LABOUR'S LOST

The rose appears all through Shakespeare's works. Sixty references extol the beauties of the queen of flowers. The roses of his time that were most sweet and poetical were the red rose, the white rose, the damask, and the musk rose. The first two are native to England; the latter was brought to English gardens from North Africa, its home, or from Italy in the time of Henry VIII. Eglantine, or sweetbrier (*Rosa eglanteria*), a rose with fragrant leaves, so much a part of every English garden, adorns Titania's bower

Other roses of Shakespeare's time were the cabbage rose (*Rosa centifolia*); the damask rose (*R. damascena*), a native of Syria but grown in English gardens since 1270 and much used for rose jars, sweet baths, and perfume; and the wild or dog rose of the hedges (*R. canina*). The dog rose was so named by the Romans, who used the root to cure the bite of mad dogs. It was once believed that the crown of thorns was made from this rose. The variegated rose, or damask, known as York and Lancaster, with pink and white petals on the same flower, is typical of Tudor gardens. (*R. gallica* 'versicolor' with striped red and white flowers is often mistaken for the variegated damask of Shakespeare's time.)

Not only were roses grown for scent and beauty in the garden, but the flowers were systematically gathered to make essences, sweet bags, and rose jars to perfume the house. Rose syrup was used as a cordial, and rose petals were made into jam and were candied for decorations. Rose water was used to wash in. So great was the commercial demand that the dried roses were imported from Constantinople.

> *The Rose looks fair, but fairer it we deem*
> *For that sweet odor which doth in it live. . . .*
> *But for their virtue only is their show,*
> *They live unwoo'd and unrespected fade;*
> *Die unto themselves. Sweet roses do not so;*
> *Of their sweet deaths are sweetest odors made.*
> SONNET 54

> *A rose by any other name would smell*
> *as sweet.*
> ROMEO AND JULIET

Roses have long been a part of history and legend. Venus is crowned with roses, her flower, and she in turn decked her perpetually youthful son Cupid with rose garlands. The God of Silence received a rose from Cupid, and the flower became the symbol of silence and secrecy.

The brides of Greece and Rome were decked with crowns and garlands of the rose. Wine was flavored with it, and jellies and jams made from it. The Romans dedicated the red rose to Jupiter. Damask and white roses became the flowers of Diana, or the Rose of the Moon. The rose became the Christian symbol of the Virgin Mary, the white rose symbolizing purity; the red rose represents the blood of martyrs. Rosaries are said to have been made originally of pressed rose petals.

Rosemary   *Rosmarinus officinalis*

> *Reverend sir, for you there's*
> *   Rosemary and Rue; these keep*
> *Seeming and savour all the winter*
> *   long.*
>   WINTER'S TALE

> *There's Rosemary, that's for*
> *   remembrance; pray you love,*
> *   remember.*
>   HAMLET

> *Dry up your tears, and stick your*
> *   Rosemary*
> *On this fair corse.*
>   ROMEO AND JULIET

Rosemary was a plant of marked importance in Shakespeare's time. It was considered decorative by the landscape gardeners and by gentlemen gardeners of Bacon's stature. Parkinson speaks of its popularity as a garden plant:

> Being in every woman's garden, it were sufficient but to name it as an ornament among other sweet herbs and

flowers in our gardens. In this our land, where it hath been planted in noblemen's and great men's gardens against brick walls, and there continued long, it riseth up in time unto a very great height, with a great and woody stem of that compasse that, being cloven out into boards, it hath served to make lutes or such like instruments, and here with us carpenters' rules and to divers others purposes. . . . Rosemary is almost of as great use as Bayes, both for civill as physicall purposes—inwardly for the sinews and joynts; for civill uses, as all do know, at weddings, funerals, and to bestow among friends.

Rosemary is the plant that delights in sea spray and is therefore called *Rosmarinus*, or dew of the sea.

Rue   *Ruta graveolens*

> *How did she fall a tear, here in this place*
> *I'll set a bank of Rue, sour herb of Grace*
> *But, even for ruth, here shortly shall be seen,*
> *In the remembrance of a weeping queen.*
>
> RICHARD II

A bank of rue in the Shakespeare garden is a joy. Its blue green, cut leaves change little with the seasons. Rue, in England, was called the judge's plant, for it was either suspended over the judges' heads to protect them from jail fever when they were sentencing prisoners or was put into nosegays and laid on either the judge's desk or the book of laws. Bunches of rue were used to sprinkle holy water in the churches. It was also used as an expression of regret, as in "to rue the day."

Samphire   *Crithmum martimum*

> *Half-way down*
> *Hangs one that gathers Samphire*
> *   dreadful trade!*
> *Methinks he seems no bigger than*
> *   his head.*
>
> KING LEAR

This fleshy pungent herb with leaves like small hands thrives in the rocks of England's seacoast, where it clambers down over the cliffs, growing just above the wash of the water. In some areas it has spread into the surrounding meadows; it may also be grown in the garden. "Samphire" is a contraction of Saint Pierre, or Saint Peter, for whom the plant was named, in accordance with its association with the rocks. In Shakespeare's day samphire was a popular pickle. The leaves were put in brine and became "the pleasantest sauce, most familiar, and best agreeing with man's body."

Savory

Satureja hortensis (Summer)
S. montana (Winter)

> *Here's flowers for you,*
> *Hot Lavender, sweet Mints, Savory,*
> *Marjoram.*
>
> WINTER'S TALE

The various savories were favorite plants of Shakespeare's day and were mentioned by Parkinson as stuffing herbs. Winter savory is a decorative herb that grows like a small shrub, developing a woody stem as it matures. We have used it to advantage as a border for a culinary garden, and again in the planted wall of the Shakespeare garden. Here it trails gracefully over the edge of the gray stones and produces white flowers like tiny drops of dew. It is hardy, and the small first-year plants become large spreading shrubs in the second and third years.

Strawberry

Fragaria vesca

> *Have you not sometimes seen a handkerchief*
> *Spotted with Strawberries in your wife's hand?*
>
> OTHELLO

> *The Strawberry grows beneath the Nettle,*
> *And wholesome berries thrive and ripen best*

Neighbored by fruit of lesser quality;
And on the prince obscured his contemplation
Under the veil of wilderness.

HENRY V

Fragaria vesca is a native of Europe that has naturalized in the United States. It is a creeping plant with tiny white blossoms and red or white fruits.

Thyme   *Thymus serpyllum*

I know a bank where the wild
Thyme grows.
MIDSUMMER NIGHT'S DREAM

We will plant Nettles or sow Lettuce,
set Hyssop and weed up Thyme.

OTHELLO

Thyme and its many varieties are such an integral part of the herb garden that we cannot imagine planning a planting without it. It was once used by the Greeks and Romans as incense in sacrifices from whence it received its name *thymon*. This was later introduced into the English language as thyme. Serpyllum refers to its creeping habit.

Violet, Sweet   *Viola odorata*

Violets dim
and sweeter than the lids of Juno's
eyes
Or Cythera's breath.
WINTER'S TALE

To throw a perfume on the violet
Is wasteful and ridiculous excess.
KING JOHN

[105]

The yellows, blues,
The purple violets and marigolds
Shall as a carpet hang upon thy
    grave
While summer days do last.
                            PERICLES

The English violet is well known among flowers for its sweetness, but all members of the viola family are lovely additions to
the Shakespeare garden. Violets act as a ground cover in shady
areas and grow happily with sweet woodruff and sweet cicely. We
grow white, pink (*Rosina*), and purple (*Viola tricolor*) to carry
the bloom through the month of May. The blossoms are used in
punch, particularly May wine. Both blossoms and leaves are an
interesting and healthful addition to salads.

Wormwood   *Artemisia absinthium*
        To weed this Wormwood from your
            fruitful brain.
                        LOVE'S LABOUR'S LOST

        For I had then laid Wormwood to
            my dug.
        When it did taste the Wormwood on
            the nipple
        Of my dug, and felt it bitter,
            pretty fool.
                        ROMEO AND JULIET

"As bitter as wormwood" has long been descriptive of this
handsome member of the artemisia family. It has always enjoyed
a high reputation in folk medicine and is famous for its use in the
manufacture of absinthe. Today it may be used as an herbal moth
preventive, in veterinarian medicines, in bitters, and as a tonic
if taken under careful supervision.

[106]

5
A Garden of the Saints

FOR CENTURIES THE association of religion and solitude, of nature and art, of plants and God, led holy men, laity, and repentant sinners into the wilderness to build shrines. Some of these recluses were satisfied with nature as it was and made no gardens of their own. They lived in caves and fought their devils in solitude. Others, feeling sorrow for the ills of their fellowmen, found ways to cure the sick of mind and body with the wild herbs that grew nearby. Communities developed around these healers, and gardens were cultivated. Monasteries furnished food for the hungry body, as well as calm for the tortured soul, and so the gardens grew and the number of plants multiplied. Thus gardening became an important part of monastic life.

These refugees from the cares of the world initiated inquiries into medical science and, having leisure to study, preserved and promoted intellectual pursuits. Not all were adept at illuminating manuscripts or writing tracts. Some were physicians of the body as well as of the soul; others saw miracles in the growth of a seed or the grafting of a tree. Many among them lived and died in the anonymity of their order, but produced new fruits or discovered better ways of using the products of the land. Many, too, were enthralled with the sweet odors and the beauty of flowers and leaves. They contributed to their faith by growing plants for the decoration of shrines and altars. It was possible to step from the church sanctuary into a small green world called paradise, where these plants were grown.

Mary gardens became a part of many monastery enclosures. In these sheltered spots were planted the trees, flowers, and herbs that bore Mary's name or were associated with her in truth or legend. As the veneration of Mary grew, secular as well as church gardens were dedicated to her. The number of plants that bore her name also increased as travelers brought offerings from remote parts of the world.

Interest in these gardens of symbolism diminished as people took a more prosaic approach to gardening. Plant histories were relegated to neglected, dusty volumes in old libraries. Eventually, in our time, the pendulum swung back, and serious effort is now being made to re-create these peaceful gardens of the past. Statues of the holy people, who worked with the plants that grew along monastery walls, are finding their way into our gardens again, to accompany the plants they tended or those that have since been dedicated to them.

In these green retreats we place statues of the saints whose lives have some connection with gardening, flowers, birds, bees, forestry, husbandry, harvest, and medicine. Their very names ring like Gothic bells: Saint Francis of Assisi; Saint Fiacre of Scotia; Saint Phocas of Sinope; Saint Giles of Aegidius, famous for his love of animals; and Saint Dorothea of Caesarea for roses. All of these, and various others, are appropriate in a Garden of the Saints.

GARDEN OF THE SAINTS

Our garden has three shrines. Against a weathered wood fence of gray chestnut boards is a terra-cotta statue of the Virgin and Child. The statue has taken on a wonderful look of age with its exposure to the elements. Mary has become a dreaming figure in a world of muted colors, sweet odors, and shy blossoms. Behind her, almost covering the fence, is the hop vine, which reminds us of the brew house in the monastery industry. Nearby are rosemary plants, with their fragrant, needlelike leaves and small, mostly blue flowers. Most of the other plants around Mary are white, to symbolize her purity. There are the "violet of humility," the white or blue white iris so often used in celebrations of the annunciation, and the handsome and stately madonna lily whose pure white blossoms represent virginity and innocence.

In the center of the garden and leading directly to the Mary figure is a flat, elongated cross of stone. The stone is planted with a variety of thymes, manger herbs. The creeping thymes have numerous leaf shapes and colors. They are fragrant with tiny flowers that are lavender, blue, or white.

To the left, as we face the statue of the Virgin Mary, is a terra-cotta Saint Fiacre, one of the few holy people who actually cultivated the soil. In France Saint Fiacre has long been recognized as the patron saint of gardeners, and in the last decade he has become the patron saint of many American gardeners as well. A prim little stone path leads to Saint Fiacre's shrine. Around him are some treasured plants of monastery gardens and medicinal plants that commemorate the work of the monks in healing the sick.

[109]

There are salvias. This botanical name of the sages means "save" and refers to the innumerable medicinal uses our ancestors devised for the plants. Its green gray leaves and blue, pink, or white flowers make it a decorative addition to any garden. The myrtle tree, on the other side of Saint Fiacre, is a common plant of Palestine and Bethlehem. True myrtle has fragrant, dark, evergreen leaves, white to pink flowers, and blue black fruits. In biblical references it is a symbol of peace, joy, and justice.

Our statue of Saint Fiacre has him resting on a spade, reminding us that gardening is hard and meticulous work, for the ground must be cultivated, the seeds sown, weeds pulled, and plants kept neat and trim. This is not a task for one who is only a mystic, but for one who combines labor and prayer.

Saint Francis, best known and most loved of the saints, occupies a place somewhat removed from the garden, for il Poverello, as he is known, did not cultivate the soil, though he loved all of nature. In thousands of shrines throughout the world he is seen giving his blessings to the birds and the beasts. He sang hymns and canticles to the sun and to the birds, calmed the wild beasts, and protected all natural things, loving all nature as a gift of God. In our garden a tall, terra-cotta figure of the saint stands in a rough stone wall. Before him is a large, flat rock that is covered with *vinca minor*. Its shining leaves make a dark green carpet around his feet. In early spring the carpet is covered with the familiar blue flowers. A hollowed stone nearby forms a bath for the birds he loved so much.

In our search for the plants appropriate for a garden of the saints we found that we were living in a medieval past where an aura of romance, as well as of religion, colored stories and descriptions of the ancient gardens. Were these tales superstitions, were they based on facts, or just mere fancies? This is not important to those of us who find it well worthwhile to immerse ourselves in an atmosphere completely at variance with our scientific world.

Symbolism, which bears an air of preciousness to many practical people, persists in a realistic world. It lives on in all the arts, in painting, in song and story, in all church rituals. The ancient symbols persist, and throughout the ages they have touched the heart and the imagination with the gentle hands of poetry.

Saints of the Out-of-Doors

Our Garden of the Saints enshrines the Virgin Mary, Saint Francis, and Saint Fiacre, but the lives of several other saints were in many ways connected with the out-of-doors. They tilled the land, spent their time in the fields and forests, protected birds and beasts, planted gardens, or used plants for devotion or healing. Any of these holy people may well be enshrined in a garden. Saints Dorothea, Elizabeth, Giles, Isidore, Maurilius, Phocas, Serenius, or Thérèse might well be the ones to whom you dedicate your garden.

Saint Francis of Assisi

Saint Francis was born Francesco Bernardone in 1181 or 1182. He grew up in luxury, the son of a rich cloth merchant. Francis was a wild and talented youth, much in demand among his companions for his singing, clowning, and high spirits. The usual escapades of youth led to battles with the authorities and resulted in his confinement in prison. After regaining his freedom, he suffered a severe illness, during which he underwent a complete spiritual transformation that resulted in a desire for a life of poverty and worship. He gave away his rich clothes and jewels and refused all charity except enough to care for one day at a time. His days were spent in prayer, fasting, and preaching.

In 1209 a few disciples joined him, forming the nucleus of the Brothers Minor. They lived in abject poverty, laying aside nothing for the future. They slept in caves or rude huts and rejected all man-made comforts. Francis shared what little food he had with the birds and animals, calling them his brothers. The sun was his brother, also. All the elements, even the bitter sleet that cut through

[111]

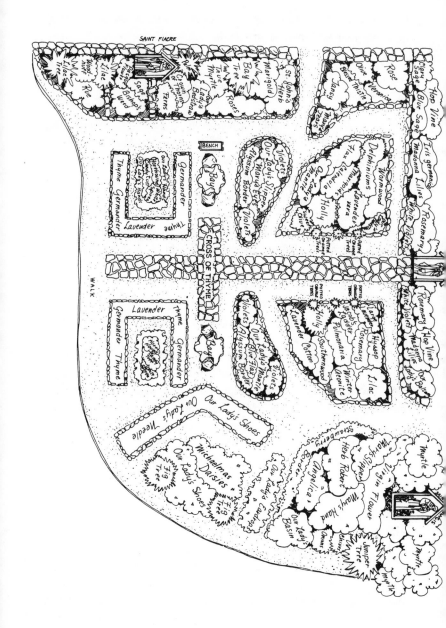

his thin garments and the deep snow that froze his sandaled feet, were loved by him as a part of the great world of God.

The order of the Brothers Minor grew, and Francis was urged to establish a definite rule for the growing number of "Little Brothers," the men who, inspired by his preaching, his honesty, and his saintly magnetism, were moved to follow him in the way of poverty. In 1212 the order of the Sisters of the Poor was established with Clare of Assisi at its head. About 1221 a third order was formed for lay people who desired to live the religious life while still working in the world.

In 1221 Francis was displaced as head of the Franciscans, and the direction of his order passed into other hands. A small group of his devoted followers remained around him, and his life of prayer, preaching, and praise went on. The culmination of his life came when he received the stigmata marks of the wounds suffered by Christ on the cross. Three years after this, on October 3, 1226, Saint Francis knew his work was at an end. Resting on the bare earth, he sang his way into the arms of death. The Franciscan order grew and became one of the most popular and powerful religious organizations in the world.

Saint Francis is usually depicted dressed in brown sackcloth with a rope sash, and with bare or sandaled feet. A bird may sit in his hand or on his shoulder, or a wolf may walk by his side.

Saint Fiacre

Saint Fiacre was born a prince in Scotia on May 1, 590. His father was Lord Coleman, a heathen influenced by the druids. His mother, Lady Brigida, was a devout Christian. Since Fiacre was to succeed his father in ruling the kingdom, the youth was trained in battle and intrigue. But the young Fiacre followed his mother's religion, his gentler interests fostered by her faith and teaching.

The death of his mother left Fiacre in surroundings uncongenial to his religious tastes, and to satisfy his religious beliefs, he left home to enter a monastery. After some years of monastic life he went to France. There a bishop offered him a tract of land where he might establish a retreat for prayer and contemplation. Half in jest, the bishop said he could have as much land as he could entrench in a single day. Fiacre, prayerfully walking on the uncultivated land, came upon a glade that seemed just right for his purpose. He raised his staff and walked forward, his lips moving in prayer. A great furrow miraculously appeared, stones were turned aside, and bushes were uprooted as he advanced. A tract of land great enough for a garden and a church was surrounded.

This miracle was observed by a peasant woman who believed that she had witnessed the work of the devil. She went in haste and fear to the bishop, who followed her to the spot. There he saw a clearing where fresh dark furrows made a sacred enclosure. On the moist earth knelt the young monk in an ecstasy of devotion. The bishop, without further questioning, gave his blessing that the good work of Fiacre might begin.

Fiacre followed the miracle with years of earnest labor. In his garden he produced herbs for healing and flowers for beauty. As time went by, his place became famous, for he treated the sick with his herbs and the unhappy with his wisdom. In the sixty years that he lived at Brie, his desire for a hermit's life was not realized. So great was his fame as a healer and holy man that a community grew up around him, and his chapel, dedicated to the Virgin Mary, became the shrine of many worshipers.

Saint Fiacre is shown as an elderly man with a long white beard. He usually carries a book or a flower and a long-handled spade.

PLANTS FOR THE GARDEN
OF THE SAINTS

In selecting plants that might be included in a garden dedicated to the Virgin Mary and the saints we have found many herbs associated with the feast days of particular saints or in some way associated with their lives. Others were chosen because they were raised in monastery gardens or were used in early religious ceremonies. Some, like the "Mary" or "Our Lady" plants, have symbolic representation. Others were chosen for their color. White flowers, for example, symbolize the purity of Mary and predominate in gardens dedicated to the Virgin.

Aconite, Winter   *Eranthis hyemalis cilicica*
Winter aconite is a hardy, tuberous plant that grows to eight inches and bears yellow flowers in the very early spring.

Alyssum, Sweet   *Lobularia maritima*
The self-sowing plants of sweet alyssum will quickly come up from seed and produce mounds of fragrant white blossoms that last until the snows come. They are as fragrant as their name implies.

Barberry   *Berberis vulgaris*
Barberry, used in the celebrations of Saint Columba's Day, is a deciduous shrub bearing clusters of small yellow flowers in spring. The foliage turns reddish in fall when the bright red berries appear.

Bay Tree, Sweet Bay   *Laurus nobilis*
Laurus nobilis, a beautiful shrub or tree with dark green, fragrant leaves, is associated with Saint Lucian. This is not the common laurel of our woodlands (*Kalmia latifolia*), which is poisonous. In the United States *Laurus nobilis* is a pot-grown plant and is wintered indoors. In its native Mediterranean habitat it is a tree growing to forty feet in height, with dark, glossy, green leaves, yellow flowers, and black or dark purple fruits. This is the bay tree of the Bible.

Bishop's Weed   *Aegopodium podagraria*
This native of Europe, naturalized in the United States, is a creeping plant with clusters of small yellow or white flowers. The

variegated (*variegata*) form, with white markings on the leaves, is less likely to overrun adjacent plants, so is better for patterned gardens.

Bitter Herbs

Five bitter herbs are recorded as being eaten with the Pascal lamb: endive, lettuce, chicory, cress, and dandelion. Sorrel and horehound were also included and eaten with the others as salad. Dandelion, one of the bitter herbs eaten at Passover feasts, was used as a symbol of the passion. A bitter cup given as a form of anesthetic included gall, myrrh, wormwood, and horehound.

Candytuft   *Iberis sempervirens*

An evergreen, candytuft forms a low cushion of lustrous green leaves. In spring it is covered with clusters of small white flowers.

Chive   *Allium schoenoprasum*

Chive is a handsome plant of ancient religious significance, with cylindrical, hollow leaves and almost ball-like clusters of tiny flowers on single stems. It is usually cultivated for its onion-flavored leaves, but some varieties are forced by florists for early spring flowers. 'Ruby Gem' has gray foliage and pink ruby flowers.

Fig Tree   *Ficus carica*

The fig tree was revered by Christians as the fruit asked for by Jesus on the way to Bethany. It is a symbol of peace, life, and knowledge. The common fig tree is a deciduous plant that grows to thirty feet under favorable, close to tropical, conditions. In most of the United States it is grown as a shrub in a tub and wintered inside. If properly protected, it will bear edible fruit even in the North.

Flax   *Linum perenne*
                                    L. usitatissimum

For centuries, flax was the only universal textile fabric, and a failure of the crop was of serious concern. Because of the people's dependence upon this harvest, it became the central motif in many festivals. This oldest of textile fibers was known and used in the land of Canaan before the Israelites. Linen was used by the Hebrews as the winding sheet for their dead, and the body of Jesus was wrapped in linen after the Crucifixion.

Both the annual (perenne) and perennial (usitatissimum) flax are well worth growing for the enjoyment of the delicate blue flowers that nod on long stems.

Germander *Teucrium lucidum*

Germander is important in the border. It was a favorite edging plant in Elizabethan gardens and still may be seen at Hampton Court. For patterned gardens or when used as a border it is best to cut the spikes of red purple flowers that rise above the leaves, leaving only the stiff foliage.

Herb Robert *Geranium robertianum*
Wild Geranium

The wild geranium, with its red purple flowers, is often found growing in shady, moist woodlands. It is commonly thought to be named after Saint Robert, who is credited with halting a plague that swept England by treating the disease with the little red-stemmed plant.

Herb Trinity *Viola tricolor*
Our Lady's Delight
Heart's-Ease
Johnny-jump-up
Pansy

These delightful little pansies are so appealing that they would make every garden a little holier for their presence. The three petals of the flower are said to represent the Father, Son, and Holy Ghost.

Holly, English *Ilex aquifolium*

Holly has been part of religious rites and festivals since Roman times. It was used in the decoration of English Christian churches from the time of Henry VI, symbolizing eternal life. Holly is also said to be the wood of the cross.

Holy Ghost Plant   *Angelica archangelica*
This fast-growing plant is associated with the annunciation, when the three archangels, Saint Michael, Saint Gabriel, and Saint Raphael, appeared to the Virgin Mary. It was grown in monastery gardens as a medicine and flavoring agent. In the cold north it performed an important service to man as a winter food and a green medicine, rendering invaluable aid in the prevention of scurvy. Angelica is gigantic when full grown. It may reach the astonishing height of seven feet in the second year. It is best planted well back in the garden where it will be a very bold accent.

Hop Vine   *Humulus lupulus*
The hop vine is included in this garden as a reminder of the beer- and wine-making industries of monasteries. These rapidly growing vines will quickly make excellent screens if they are provided with support. The flowers of both the male and female plants are greenish yellow. The female plants bear the hops used in brewing.

Horehound   *Marrubium vulgare*
Horehound was part of the bitter cup that was given as a form of anesthesia. The name comes from the Hebrew word for bitter juice, *marrob*. The wrinkled, hoary, almost white leaves form very attractive rosettes in their early stages. The small white or purple flowers are usually cut off so that the rather unattractive burrs do not form.

Hyssop   *Hyssopus officinalis*
The hyssop of modern gardens is of European origin and not the biblical hyssop. We symbolically include in our saints' garden the modern plant that bears the name. Its bushlike habit of growth, glossy green leaves, and usually deep blue blossoms make it one of the most decorative plants in the garden.

[118]

Iris, White   *Iris germanica florentina*

White iris, flowering almond, and white narcissus are all used in the celebration of the feast of the annunciation. *Iris germanica florentina*, from which orris root is obtained, is especially handsome. It blossoms early with a large blue white flower.

Jacob's Ladder   *Polemonium caeruleum*

Jacob's ladder was used to decorate church altars on Ascension Day. Its drooping clusters of attractive blue flowers rise above deeply cut leaves in June. The plants are attractive in the garden border.

Juniper   *Juniperus*

The juniper tree of legend opened its branches to enclose the Holy Family when it was fleeing from Herod's soldiers. It became a soft bed on the inside and grew prickles like spears on the outside to repulse the pursuers. Juniper is often used in the south of Europe for decoration because of its religious associations.

Larkspur   *Delphinium ajacis*
                                                          D. belladonna
                                                          D. grandiflorum

Larkspur was one of the flowers used in the ceremonies of Saint John's Eve. It was reputed to benefit the eyes of those who looked at the ceremonial fires. The deeply cut, almost featherlike leaves and clusters of blue flowers make this plant a handsome addition to any garden.

Lavender   *Lavandula hetrophylla*
                                                          L. dentata
                                                          L. spica
                                                          L. vera

Lavender is reputed to be one of the plants most loved by the Virgin Mary, for it represented in ancient times, as it does now, purity, cleanliness, and virtue. Churches were decorated with lavender on Saint Barnabas Day. *L. vera* is the "true" lavender of which other lavenders are varieties. *L. hetrophylla* has highly scented foliage and spikes of pale blossoms through most of the summer. Gray and green *L. dentata* provides a variety of leaf and color. *L. spica*, with its thick and felty gray leaves, grows more quickly than *L. vera*, but its tall spikes of flowers are not so fragrant.

Lavender Cotton. See Santolina, Gray (page 127).

Leek *Allium porrum*

The leek is associated with Saint David, the patron saint of Wales, who was said to have lived almost exclusively on a diet of leeks. The saint appeared to King Arthur after the King's men had been saved from starvation by eating the plentiful plant. Leeks are decorative enough for any garden, especially when they attain full height and put on their fantastic caps of seeds.

Lilac *Syringa vulgaris*

This large shrub bears dense clusters of white, lavender, or deep purple flowers in late spring. They fill the air with sweet fragrance.

Lungwort *Pulmonaria officinalis*

The flowers are said to be the weeping eyes of Mary. They are blue, like eyes, and pink, like lids swollen with weeping. This is a plant of the Crucifixion.

Madonna Lily *Lilium candidum*

This stately plant is associated with the Virgin, the angel Gabriel, and Saints Dominic, Francis, and Clare. The pure white blossom represents virginity and innocence. It is the symbol of the Annunciation and the Visitation. This lily is also used in representations of the Resurrection.

Marigold *Calendula officinalis*

The marigold, once known as Marygold, was used as a church decoration on the feast of the Annunciation. It received its name of calenda, for calendar, from the fact that in its native home it was in bloom on every one of Mary's festive days. This is one of the golden plants that represent the sun, a symbol of the sun of righteousness driving out the darkness of sin. We surround the taller, later-blooming calendulas with a border of the dwarf *Tagetes pumila*, the lemon-scented marigold. It forms fine bushes which are covered with myriads of bright orange or yellow blossoms. They bloom profusely from June until November and will continue to bloom in the house if wintered indoors.

Mary's Eyes   *Myosotis sylvatica*
Forget-me-not

These charming plants are covered with rich blue flowers in April and May. There are white and pale pink varieties, but it is the blue one that is called Mary's eyes.

Mary's Hand   *Potentilla nepalensis*
Five Fingers
Potentilla

This potentilla has showy rose red flowers in clusters on long stems in midsummer. The slim leaves are hairy.

Mary's Slipper   *Aconitum napellus*
Monkshood

The deep purple blossoms of Mary's slipper appear in autumn. This showy garden plant has cut and divided leaves.

Michaelmas Daisy   *Aster* varieties
Aster, Starwort

The michaelmas daisies are known as the flowers of Saint Michael, because they bloomed on his day in England. They bear odorless flowers in many colors during late summer and fall and are related to a South African herb the Greeks used in altar decorations.

Myrtle Tree *Myrtus communis*

Throughout the history of the Greeks and Romans, myrtle was a symbol of love and immortality and a sign of success in crowns for poets and authors. Like the rose and many evergreens, it was at one time in disfavor among the early church fathers because of its association with pagan rituals. It came to be an emblem of peace, joy, and justice and is used in burial ceremonies as a symbol of immortality. Myrtle is a handsome plant with fragrant dark green leaves, which sometimes attains a height of twenty or thirty feet in warm climates. It is best wintered inside in cold climates. It grows very slowly, and a large bush is really a treasure.

Olive, Sweet *Osmanthus fragrans*

We include the sweet olive in the garden as a highly symbolic olive tree. The true olive is difficult to procure here. This semitropical tree must be wintered indoors. The olive branch is a symbol of peace. Olive oil is known as virgin oil and represents grace and purity. The richness of the oil symbolizes the providence of God toward His children. A dove carrying an olive branch is used to indicate that the dead have found new and everlasting life. In another representation an olive branch is carried to the Virgin Mary by the angel Gabriel at the time of the Annunciation.

Orange Tree *Citrus mitis calamondin*

The orange tree appears in many paintings of the Virgin Mary to represent purity, chastity, and generosity. The fragrant, waxy, white blossom is the traditional flower of the virgin bride.

In most of the United States orange trees must be grown in tubs and wintered inside. With the proper care, they produce blossoms unmatched for fragrance.

Our Lady's Balsam *Chrysanthemum balsamita*
Bible Leaf
Costmary

Costmary is best known in New England as Bible leaf, for it was, and is, used to mark favorite passages in Bibles and prayer books. This use was suggested by the long, narrow shape of the leaf. It pressed well, was fragrant, and stayed green in color. Leaves were also taken to church to chew, in the hope that their mintlike flavor would keep parishioners awake during the long sermons. The plant, in its role as Our Lady's balsam, was believed to have been used by the Virgin Mary as a healing ointment. This mint-scented member of the chrysanthemum family will quickly form a tall background of light green, fragrant leaves. It is hardy and multiplies rapidly, but it is not hard to control.

Our Lady's Basin   *Dipsacus sylvestris*
Teasel

Teasel is dedicated to Saint Blaise, the bishop of Cappadocia in the first century. He was interested in the work of the makers of woolen clothes, who formed a large part of his congregation, and devised a process of carding wool with teasel that shortened their labors. Teasels grow with pockets where the leaves join the stems, which gives rise to the name Our Lady's basin. These pockets collect rain and dew which were once considered valuable waters to beautify the skin.

Our Lady's Bedstraw   *Galium verum*
Yellow Bedstraw

It is said that in the hour when the Christ Child was born, the white blossoms of bedstraw surrounding Mary, used as a manger herb, turned to gold with His radiance. The fragrance and golden color of bedstraw flowers make the plant a welcome addition to the June garden.

Our Lady's Eardrops   *Fuchsia hybrida*

The graceful, drooping flowers of *Fuchsia hybrida* come in white, rose, yellow, or purple, with a crimson calyx.

Our Lady's Fern   *Athyrium filix-femina*

The bright green fronds of Our Lady's fern are deeply cut and measure up to three feet long.

Our Lady's Hair   *Adiantum pedatum*
Maidenhair Fern

In Wales, on Corpus Christi, the Thursday following Trinity, it was the custom to strew a kind of fern before the doors of houses. This was called Mary's fern and probably was our maidenhair fern.

Our Lady's Hand   *Lamium maculatum*

This is a low-growing, decorative herb with green and white foliage and purple or white flowers. The white markings on the leaves suggest the fingers of a hand.

Our Lady's Mantle   *Alchemilla vulgaris*

Our Lady's mantle is a perennial herb with large, gray green, pleated leaves and delicate yellow flowers in summer. The leaves, which resemble a cloak or mantle, are covered with tiny hairs that give them a shimmering look. These hairs hold drops of dew which glisten like diamonds on Mary's cape.

Our Lady's Milk Thistle   *Silybum marianum*

The leaves of this thistle are a very decorative green and white. They are said to be milk-spotted from the drops that fell from Mary's breasts as she fed the infant Jesus. The prickly five-foot stems carry large prickly leaves and thistlelike flowers of rosy purple.

Our Lady's Needle   *Artemisia pontica*
Roman Wormwood

This is a delicate gray, lacelike herb that is effective in the garden and in flower arrangements. It is a good border plant until it achieves full growth, then it may need trimming.

Our Lady's Shoes   *Aquilegia vulgaris*
Columbine

Columbine has a spurred flower; because of its resemblance to a dove, it has been used to signify the Holy Ghost. The name "columbine" comes from *columba*, the Latin word for dove.

Our Lady's Slipper *Impatiens balsamina*

The common annual balsam blossoms profusely throughout the summer with exquisite, roselike flowers. The blossoms are red, pink, rose, violet, purple, and white. New varieties of this old-fashioned plant are now available.

Pasque Flower *Anemone coronaria*
Poppy-flowered Anemone *A. pulsatilla*

The idea of immortality clings to this fragile flower that was once used to decorate the altars of the Greeks and the Romans. It was called the Flower of the Pasque, or the Flower of Easter, and is said to have been used for Easter garlands for cattle. *Anemone coronaria* is poppy-flowered, sometimes called the blood drops of Christ, for it was said to have been growing at the foot of the cross and to have been stained with blood. In the East this colorful flower has always been associated with death or grief and was much used in burial ceremonies.

Rose *Rosa rugosa (Red)*
R. eglanteria

Old parish records tell us that decorating the churches with roses was customary on Saint Barnabas Day. Our shrub roses are most like those used then. The eglantine, or sweet brier, rose is a shrubby climber with large pink flowers. Rugosa bears even larger flowers in red and white. In Christian symbolism the red rose represents martyrdom and the white rose purity. The flower was said to have grown originally without thorns in paradise, but after the fall of man it developed thorns as a reminder of his fall from grace. The Virgin Mary is called a rose without thorns because she was exempt from original sin.

Rosemary *Rosmarinus*

Rosemary, dearly beloved of herbs, was cultivated in monastery gardens for medicine and food. It was used for strewing, so that sweet odors might arise as the branches were walked upon, and was burned as an incense for fumigation. It served to drive away pestilence, and bunches of rosemary were sold on the streets of London as a protection from plague. Gilded bouquets of the herb were carried to church by bridesmaids. It was carried at funerals by the mourners, and a piece of it was thrown into the grave as a symbol of immortality and remembrance.

Rue   *Ruta graveolens*

Rue is the ancient herb of grace and also the symbol of mourning and sorrow. Like lavender, it is an herb of virtue. Bunches of rue were used to sprinkle holy water on a kneeling congregation. It was used for good luck, to drive the evil spirits away, and as a protection from the plague and infection. For some it was a symbol of virginity. The blue green leaves are a valuable addition to the texture and color of the garden. The yellow flowers come and go, giving fine color when the plants are massed together.

Sage, Blue   *Salvia officinalis*
Sage, Clary   *S. sclarea*

The word "salvia" means to save, and the efficiency of sage was proved in so many medicinal ways that it brought about the saying "How can a man die if he have sage in his garden?" It is sometimes called sage the savior and was planted on graves as a symbol of immortality. The ordinary blue culinary sage makes a handsome border plant. Its greenish gray leaves are as decorative as they are flavorsome. The lovely blue flowers attract bees and hummingbirds. Clary sage is an attractive biennial sometimes known as vatican sage. Its pink or white flowers are enhanced by the accompanying bracts in the same colors.

St. John's-wort   *Artemisia vulgaris*
Mugwort

St. John's-wort was regarded as a magic herb and used to cure many ills. Special ceremonies attended the picking of this handsome wild flower. It was blessed and hung up on doors and windows as a protection against storms, thunder, ghosts, and evil spirits, and was carried to ward off the attacks of witches. This large, spreading plant needs lots of room and is likely to overtake weaker herbs nearby. The reddish brown seed heads that follow the yellow flowers are good in dried arrangements.

Santolina, Gray   *Santolina chamaecyparissus*
Lavender Cotton

The name of this plant comes from Latin for holy flax, *sanctum lenum*. The fine leaves of gray santolina are blue green when young, but they later turn almost white. Since it is the foliage that is most interesting, the yellow flower heads are removed or the plant trimmed just before the flowers are formed.

Southernwood   *Artemisia abrotanum*

One of the most attractive group of plants for the herb garden, the southernwood's finely divided gray leaves give off the pleasant aromas of lemon, camphor, and tangerine, which make it useful as a moth repellent. Branches of southernwood were carried to church in England to protect the bearer from infection.

Spirea, White   *Filipendula ulmaria*
Our Lady of the Meadow   *Spiraea ulmaria*
Meadow Sweet
Queen-of-the-Meadow

This tall plant has feathery leaves and bears large clusters of small white flowers. It had medicinal purposes that made it useful in monastery gardens.

Star-of-Bethlehem   *Ornithogalum umbellatum*
Mary's Tears

According to legend, these little flowers sprang up from the particles of the star of the East, when it burst and fell to the ground after guiding the wise men to the manger. The plant, with its clusters of lovely white flowers, has been naturalized in the northern states. It is a good border plant.

Strawberry, Wild *Fragaria vesca*

The three-fold leaves of strawberry are said to express the holiness of the Trinity. They are sometimes used to adorn the Virgin Mary's gowns in the richly dressed figures of southern Europe that have wardrobes for every church festival. The plant is credited with being one of the principal foods of John while he was in the wilderness. The leaves of 'Solemacher' berries are green and handsome all summer, and the bright red berries are striking throughout the growing season.

Sweet Woodruff *Asperula odorata*

Garlands of the sweet woodruff that grew so abundantly at the edges of the woods were used to decorate the churches on Whitsunday and Saint Barnabas Day. It is a lovely scented ground cover with fragrant, tiny white flowers. The plant when green has a mossy smell, but the dried leaves are sweet smelling.

Tansy *Tanacetum vulgare*

The name of this plant comes from a Greek word meaning immortality, and tansy seems in every way to wish to make itself immortal. It spreads rapidly by root and sows quantities of seeds. At one time, the leaves were used at Eastertime in the making of tansy cakes. The small, buttonlike, yellow flowers can be dried and used to decorate the house and indoor shrines.

Thistle, Blessed *Carduus benedictus*
Thorn, Blessed *Cnicus benedictus*

The thistle is a symbol of earthly sorrow and sin. It is a symbol of the Passion because of its thorny character.

Thyme *Thymus vulgaris*
T. serpyllum

According to tradition, thyme was part of the hay and straw bed of the Virgin Mary and the Christ Child. The cross of thyme in the saints' garden may include several varieties, especially the creeping ones.

Veronica   *Veronica* varieties
Speedwell
   This plant is named for Saint Veronica, who wiped the face of Jesus with her veil on the road to Calvary. A portrait of the thorn-crowned head remained imprinted on the scarf and on the flowers she was wearing.

Violet, White   *Viola incognita*
   Saint Bernard described the Virgin Mary as the violet of humility. This fragrant little flower has also been used to represent the humility of the Son of God in assuming human form.

Virgin Flower   *Vinca minor*
Periwinkle
   Virgin flower is dedicated to Mary. It is a handsome ground cover with shiny, evergreen leaves and bears lovely blue flowers in early spring.

Wormwood   *Artemisia absinthium*
   The biblical wormwoods, *Herba alba* and *Judaica*, are closely related to our *Artemisia absinthium*, which was probably grown in monastery gardens. This tall, handsome plant could be placed near the statue of Saint Fiacre, since its use in medicine has been recognized for many years.

The
Versatile
Herb

6
Garden Tinctoria:
Nature's Dye Kit

THE DYE GARDEN was planned to produce small quantities of dyeing material, but it has become our primary flower and cutting garden. Many of the dye plants, instead of presenting a utilitarian appearance, are actually colorful annuals and perennials. The colors persist throughout the gardening year, beginning in the early spring when coltsfoot brings out its dandelionlike flowers. The back border, with its yellow panicles of woad, blossoms through late May. In summer anchusa carries its tall spires of clear and brilliant blue above the yellows and golds of the annual marigolds. Then the cosmos and zinnias begin an intense display that lasts into fall.

The dye garden is a wide border with paths of old red brick that flow in curving lines through the plantings. They make an attractive pattern and provide warm color through all the seasons. A broad center walk leads to a half-circle bed where tall tansy and giant marigolds rise from a low border of sweet woodruff. The background is a weathered wood fence whose line is broken by the tall plants that lean comfortably against it.

Woad, one of the largest of the back borders, was transplanted from an old herb garden where it had spread over a waste area, filling it with a thrilling yellow green color in May. This is one of the oldest dye plants of Europe and Asia, where it was especially valued for a precious blue dye. A great quantity is needed to produce anything like the inimitable blue of indigo. A large front bed is soft with the fine foliage of Our Lady's bedstraw, which grows like a ground cover in the early part of the season. In June it stretches up and produces fragrant yellow blossoms that make a mass of golden color into July and August.

Across the walk from the bedstraw is the heavy, coarse anchusa, which undergoes a magical change as it blossoms. It has four-to-five-foot spires that, in color, rival the most brilliant delphiniums. A large bed of marigolds is bright with deep orange blossoms during most of the growing season. In sharp contrast is a planting of purple cabbage that was used as a dye plant in early America. Scotch broom provides a dramatic accent, and dyer's broom spreads its spiky branches filled with yellow pealike blossoms. Lily of the valley, one of the best dye plants, makes a thick carpet of its broad green leaves, and in May sends up delicate stalks of fragrant, white, bell-shaped flowers.

Tall and stately hollyhocks and sunflowers, together with the nearby pokeweed, add height and interest along the fence. A grove of trees and herbs too tall for the formal garden is planted just beyond the fence. All of these provide useful dye material, and some, like the sumac, provide dramatic seasonal displays.

Until recently the dye garden did not include some of the most brilliant colors and cut flowers that we are now able to enjoy. Our gardens have always been exclusively herbal, and it was a pleasant surprise to find that dyers and herb growers in Canada and England had discovered the dye potential of such glorious flowers as zinnias, cosmos, and marigolds. Now the Garden Tinctoria contains more color and has the most delightful array of flowers for cutting and enjoying of any of our gardens.

HERBS AND FLOWERS AS DYES

It is easy enough to enjoy the dye garden for its color and beauty throughout the gardening season, but it takes a little dedication to fully appreciate its potential as a source of dyes. Exploring the early uses of the dye plants can, however, be an exciting experience in itself. We tend to forget that until 1850, and the discovery of aniline dyes, people all over the world were dependent on plants and animals for their colors. There are records of a thriving trade in dye stuffs during medieval times. Much of the commerce between Europe and the East during the thirteenth and fourteenth centuries included dyes as well as the silks and spices we seem to hear so much more about. Some of the plants included in our Garden Tinctoria were included in that early commerce. Madder, weld, woad, anchusa, broom, and oak bark were in great demand centuries ago.

Mordanting. Wool is usually dyed in two stages. Before the actual coloring takes place, the wool is mordanted. This process is a treatment that makes the material receptive to the dye that will follow. The mordants—usually alum, chrome, iron, or tin—enrich

[135]

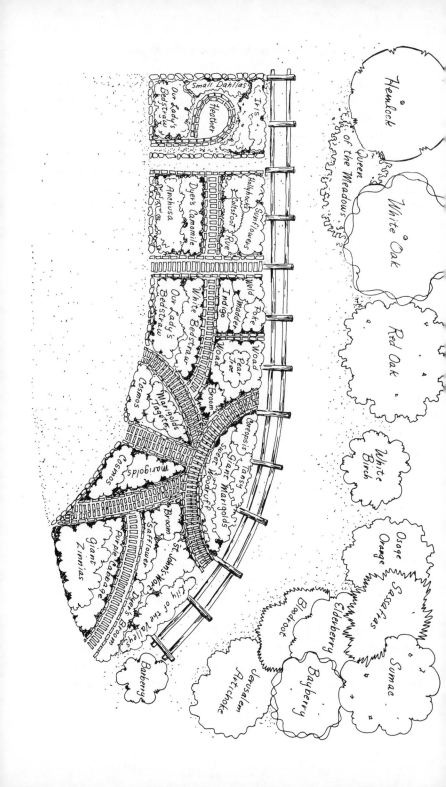

and make more permanent the colors achieved from plant materials. Some recipes for mordanting and dyeing wool are included in later descriptions of the dye plants. Where specific instructions are not given, you might try this popular method: Use a mordant including 8 ounces of alum, 2 ounces of cream of tartar, 2 pounds of white wool in skeins, and 8 gallons of water. Rinse the wool in a bath of warm water that is the same temperature as the mordanting solution. Treat the wool gently. Do not stir it around, do not wring it, do not allow it to boil. Gently place the warm and wet wool in the warm mordant and simmer it for 30 minutes. Allow the wool to cool in the mordant and rinse it in water that is the same temperature as the dye bath, being sure to avoid sudden temperature changes. Immerse the warm and wet wool in the lukewarm dye bath. Move the wool gently back and forth in the bath and simmer it for 30 minutes. Rinse the wool in water that is the same temperature as the dye bath and then in several waters that are gradually cooler. Dry in the shade.

PLANTS FOR THE
DYE GARDEN*

Anchusa   *Alkanet*

The name "anchusa" came from the Greek word for "paint for the skin." In earlier days a kind of rouge was made from it. In the garden the large clumps of hairy leaves spring forth leafy stalks bearing usually brilliant blue flowers that generally last from mid-July until September. The root of the plant produces lilac with alum and iron mordants. Red is produced with an alum mordant.

Apple   *Pyrus malus*

Apple tree bark produces a golden yellow. Soak about 2 pounds of bark pieces in water overnight and then boil them for 3 hours.

---

* Includes some plants not shown in plot plan.

Strain the liquid into a bath. Immerse alum-and-cream-of-tartar-mordanted wool in the lukewarm bath. Simmer for 30 minutes. Rinse and dry in the shade.

Barberry   *Berberis vulgaris*

Barberry shrubs are colorful additions to the dye garden, especially in the fall when their leaves turn a glowing red and they bear bright red berries. The roots and the leaves yield a yellow that is used by both wool and leather dyers. No mordant is necessary.

Bayberry   *Myrica pensylvanica*

In the wild this shrub will grow to eight or nine feet, but it can be trimmed and kept within the garden scale. The gray fruits are used in making fragrant candles; the pungent leaves for a gray green dye. Soak summer-picked leaves in water to cover for 24 hours and then boil for 1 hour. Strain the liquid into a bath. Immerse wet, alum-mordanted wool in the lukewarm bath and simmer for 30 minutes. Rinse well and dry in the shade.

Bedstraw, Our Lady's   *Galium verum*

Lady's bedstraw, a member of the madder family, is a ground cover in early spring, but later its fragrant yellow flowers rise to a height of two feet. The very small leaves, which grow in whorls, make a mass of attractive star-shaped foliage. The roots can be used to prepare a red dye, and the tops of the plants will produce yellow.

Bedstraw, White   *G. mollugo*
Wild Bedstraw (Madder)

A member of the madder family that has become naturalized in the eastern part of the United States. It bears tiny white flowers in clusters. Like the other bedstraws, it can be used to produce yellow dye from the tops of the plants and red from the roots.

Beet   *Beta*

A table vegetable that yields both red and yellow. For red, cook the beets (roots) for 1 hour and strain the resulting liquid into a bath. Immerse wool that has been mordanted in a 4-ounce alum mixture in the dye bath and simmer for 1 hour. Before rinsing, wash in soapy water. Dry in the shade. For yellow, cook the beets for 2 hours, crush them in the juice, and allow them to soak overnight. Strain the liquid into a dye bath. Immerse the wool in the bath and simmer for 30 minutes. Allow the wool to remain in the bath for an additional 2 hours before washing and rinsing. No mordant is used to make the yellow dye.

Birch, White   *Betula papyrifera*

A decoction of white birch bark will produce light brown or green. For brown, soak 1 pound of small pieces of bark in enough soft water to cover it for 10 hours. Boil the mixture for 1 hour. Strain the liquid into a bath (or soak and boil the bark in a cloth bag). Immerse washed and rinsed wool in the bath and simmer for 30 minutes. Rinse and dry. For green, follow the same procedure, but add 2 ounces of copper sulfate to the bath and simmer for 1 hour.

Bloodroot   *Sanguinaria canadensis*

Bloodroot is an Indian dye plant that grows wild in undisturbed woodlands. It was once used for war paint, to avert evil spells, and to cure arthritis. Since it takes a long time to establish a stand of bloodroot large enough to use for dye, it is probably better to include a few plants in the garden only as a reminder of the days when northern woodlands were filled with it. To prepare the red dye, cut-up roots must be soaked in water for at least 1 hour and then boiled for 30 minutes. Allow the dye mixture to cool to lukewarm and strain it into a bath of the same temperature. Place wet, alum-mordanted wool or cloth in the bath and simmer until the desired color is achieved. Rinse and dry in the shade.

[139]

Broom, Dyer's
Genista tinctoria

Masses of this Eurasian plant are found along roadsides. It transplants poorly, but it sets large amounts of seed that, with persistence, will germinate. For yellow, boil 1 pound of the yellow pealike flowers for 1 hour and strain the liquid into a bath. Immerse alum- or chrome-mordanted wool in the lukewarm bath and simmer for 1 hour. Rinse and dry in the shade.

Broom, Scotch
Cytisus scoparius

Broom is a perennial shrub with sweeping branches that may grow from six to ten feet. Different varieties may carry the fragrant, pea-shaped, usually yellow blossoms through June and July. The flowering branches yield yellow. Soak the chopped-up branches in water overnight and then boil them for 1 hour. Strain the liquid into a bath. Immerse the wool in the lukewarm bath and simmer for 1 hour. Rinse and dry in the shade. A good green is produced by using this process on wool that has been dyed with indigo.

Butternut
Juglans cinerea

Butternut and black walnut (*J. nigra*) have similar dye properties and are important in the production of deep brown and black. The properties of both trees were well known to the Indians, who shared their knowledge with the early settlers. In 1669 Massachusetts Bay Colony Governor John Winthrop sent samples of butternut-dyed material to Europe. "They dyed it," he said, "only with a decoction of the bark, without allum or copperas. Butternut bark is put into an iron kettle, and if allowed to remain long enough will dissolve enough of the iron to make a tolerable black." The uniforms of the South's Civil War soldiers were nicknamed butternuts because they had been home-dyed with the bark of this tree. Today the green hulls of butternuts are used to produce a good brown. Soak 2 pounds of the hulls in water for 12 hours. Boil them for 1 hour and strain the liquid into a bath. Immerse 1 pound of wool in the dye bath and simmer for 30 minutes. Rinse and dry in the shade. Cotton that has been mordanted first in an alum and soda solution and then in a tannic acid solution will dye gray if treated the same way as wool and then simmered with ferrous sulfate.

Cabbage, Purple   *Brassica oleracea*
Purple cabbage was one of the dye plants used by the colonists when little else was available. It is included in our garden only for its historical significance.

Coltsfoot   *Tussilago farfara*
An early-blooming, wild plant that bears heads of bright yellow flowers. It can be transplanted to the garden, but its growth must be carefully controlled. Coltsfoot spreads rapidly in sunny and dry places. The leaves produce a good green yellow. A beautiful green results from the addition of copperas.

Coreopsis   *Coreopsis tinctoria*
Calliopsis
One of the most spectacular plants for a dye garden, producing flowers of bright yellow, brown orange, and yellow with red markings from late spring until fall. Blossoms will produce brick red on wool that has been mordanted in potassium dichromate. Boil ½ bushel of flowers for 30 minutes. Strain the liquid into a bath and simmer it with the mordanted and rinsed wool until the desired shade is achieved.

Cosmos   *Cosmos* 'Sunset'
A large stand of this new variety of cosmos in bloom is a gorgeous sight, with a mass of color varying from deepest orange to an orange yellow. Of all our dye flowers, the anchusa and this cosmos attract the most attention. The cosmos makes an orange dye when chrome is used as a mordant, and a yellow one with a tin and cream of tartar mordant. Boil 2 pecks of fresh flower heads for 30 minutes. Cool the mixture to lukewarm and strain the liquid into a dye bath of the same temperature. Immerse the

wet, mordanted wool in the bath and simmer for 30 minutes. Rinse and dry in the shade.

Dahlia   *Dahlia*

The showy heads of dahlia flowers make a brilliant display of red, purple, yellow, and white in late summer and fall. The yellow flowers will produce a good orange on alum-mordanted wool and yellow on wool mordanted with chrome. Cover 2 pecks of cut-up flowers with water and boil for 20 minutes. Strain the liquid into a 4-gallon bath. Immerse the rinsed and mordanted wool in the bath and simmer for 20 minutes. Rinse and dry in the shade.

Dandelion   *Taraxacum officinale*

This major nuisance for the turf gardener yields a magenta dye. Boil the whole plant for 2 hours and strain the liquid into a bath. Immerse the wool in the lukewarm bath and simmer for 30 minutes. Rinse and dry in the shade.

Dock   *Rumex obtusifolius*

Dock is a common weed that is a menace to the farmer, invaluable to the flower arranger, and of interest to the home dyer. The leaves are long and have red veins, but these are hardly noticeable after the tall red seed heads appear. The roots of dock produce a dark yellow on alum-mordanted wool. Soak ½ pound of chopped roots in water to cover overnight. Boil for 1 hour and strain the liquid into the bath. Immerse the wet and mordanted wool in the bath and simmer for 1 hour. Rinse well and dry.

Dyer's Camomile   *Anthemis tinctoria*

We have grown this lovely golden marguerite as an excellent cutting flower for years. It adds much color to the garden, for it blooms almost constantly after its first flowering in late June. After the anchusa has lost its glorious blue flowers, the marguerite fills in the color gap. The flower heads produce yellow, khaki, and gold with different mordants. To prepare the dye, boil 1 peck of chopped flower heads for 30 minutes. Strain the liquid into a bath. For yellow, immerse wet, alum-mordanted wool in the cold dye bath. Bring to a boil and simmer for 1 hour. Rinse and dry in the shade. For khaki, immerse wet, alum-mordanted wool in the dye bath and simmer for 30 minutes. Then immerse the still hot and wet wool in another dye bath containing ⅙ ounce of potassium dichromate and ⅙ ounce of acetic acid. Simmer for 15 minutes and rinse well.

Elderberry   *Sambucus canadensis*

The wild elderberry is a tall shrub that may, at maturity, exceed six feet. Its clusters of white blossoms are among the most beautiful of wild bloom, and the bush is equally as decorative when it is hanging heavy with its dark purple fruits. Elderberry is a plant of legend and mystery. It is said to be the wood from which Christ's cross was made and that it consequently cannot be struck by lightning. In England it was used as a protection against witches. The fruits produce a good blue violet on wool that has been mordanted in 4 gallons of water containing 2 ounces of alum and 1 ounce of cream of tartar. Cook 2 pounds of the fruit for 30 minutes and strain the liquid into a bath. Immerse the wet, mordanted wool in the lukewarm bath and simmer for 30 minutes. For a deeper, more purple color, use 5 pounds of fruit and allow it to soak in water overnight before boiling.

Fustic, Young   *Rhus cotinus*
Smoke Tree   *Cotinus coggygria*

True fustic, or old fustic, is *Chlorophora tinctoria*, a large tree of the mulberry family that is a native of tropical America. Some gardeners have been successful in growing it in the United States. An extract of wood chips is used to produce yellow, green, and brown with different mordants, but most dyers buy the already prepared extract. The dedicated dyer-grower will find that the smoke tree is a good substitute even though its dye is somewhat less permanent. *Rhus cotinus rubrum*, or *purpurea*, is a most ornamental shrub. The dark, reddish purple leaves turn a kind of gray in summer, and the flowers give an aura of smoke that is spectacular. Yellow dye can be extracted from the twigs and bark.

Goldenrod   *Solidago*

Goldenrod is so easily found in fields and along roadsides that it seems unnecessary to give it space in the garden. If you want to include it, choose the lance-leafed kind, since it is the most decorative in foliage and produces almost mimosalike flowers which are excellent in dried arrangements. Yellow tan is produced with an alum mordant. Chrome makes an old gold. Cover 1½ pecks of flower heads with cold water and boil for 1 hour. Strain the liquid into the dye bath. Immerse the mordanted material in the bath and simmer for 30 minutes. Rinse well and dry in the shade.

Heather   *Calluna vulgaris*

The use of heather as a dye comes from the northern part of Europe—Norway, Sweden, and Scotland—where it grows wild in large areas of the countryside. It is new in our garden. The young branches of heather produce a good green. Boil them for 2 hours and strain the liquid into a bath. Immerse the wool in the lukewarm bath to which a small amount of alum has been added. Simmer for 30 minutes. Yellow can be extracted from the flowers and stems of heather. Boil them for 1 hour and simmer the wool in the resulting dye bath for 30 minutes. If only the flowers are used, purple is produced. The process is the same as that for the flowers and stems except that 1 ounce of alum is added to the bath for each pound of wool.

Hemlock   *Tsuga canadensis*

The reddish brown dye that can be produced from the mature bark of the hemlock has been used for leather tanning in Canada.

When alum is used as the mordant, wool takes on a permanent red brown and cotton assumes a brownish hue. With the use of copperas, drab and slate colors are produced.

Hollyhock *Althea rosea*

The hollyhock is indigenous to China. Pilgrims from the Holy Land first introduced this tall and handsome plant into Britain. The hibiscus is one of the most glamorous members of this great family. Red hollyhock flowers produce a red dye, and the leaves make a yellow green one. For the red dye, crush 1 pound of flowers and soak them in water overnight. Boil the mixture for 1 hour and strain the liquid into a 4-gallon dye bath to which ½ teaspoon of ammonia has been added. Immerse the wet, mordanted wool in the bath and simmer for 30 minutes. The mordant is 2 ounces of alum and 1 of cream of tartar for 1 pound of wool. The yellow green dye is made the same way, with 2 pounds of leaves.

Indigo, Wild *Baptisia tinctoria*

Wild indigo is found in sandy, well-drained, even impoverished soil, sometimes along roadsides where it seems to cling to rocks and a little soil. It is a pretty, well-shaped bush with tiny leaves and a mass of pealike flowers. If it were not so difficult to transplant, wild indigo would appear in many gardens just for its decorative qualities. References to the plant are found among the writings of the Dutch settlers of New York City and Albany. They apparently cultivated it; some have said it was even more profitable than cotton. Cultivation of both wild and true indigo was adandoned during the Civil War when the growth of foodstuffs became more necessary. The plant produces blue on alum-mordanted wool.

Iris *Iris*

Iris is included in our dye garden as a kind of symbolic gesture. Dyers have experimented with it here, but results of these experiments seem not to have been recorded. In Scotland the root of a wild bog iris is used to produce black.

Jerusalem Artichoke   *Helianthus tuberosus*
   Member of the sunflower family, also called Canadian potato, because of its edible root. For its use as a dye, see Sunflower (page 151).

Juniper   *Juniperus virginiana*
Red Cedar
   Juniper is one of the most decorative and traditional of the herbal trees. It is especially attractive in the fall when it bears gray blue berries. Boiled berries produce a good khaki color on wool that has been mordanted in alum, ammonium chloride, cream of tartar, and copper sulfate.

Lily of the Valley   *Convallaria majalis*
   Although only the leaves of this fragrant spring plant are used for dying, the flowers give the dye garden fragrance in spring, and the lovely white flowers are decorative if massed together. A pale greenish yellow comes from the leaves gathered in spring. Autumn leaves produce gold. The mordant is chrome. For 1 pound of wool, pick 1½ pecks of fresh leaves. Shred the leaves, soak them in water for 12 hours, and then boil them for 1 hour. Strain the liquid into a 5-gallon bath. Immerse the wool in the lukewarm bath and simmer for 45 minutes. Rinse and dry in the shade.

Madder   *Rubia tinctorum*
   Although it has frequently been imported into America and was for a long time in great demand, madder has never been grown here in great quantity. Our Lady's bedstraw, sweet woodruff, and white bedstraw are members of the same family of plants. White bedstraw, a perennial of our roadsides and meadows, is attractive enough to be included in any flower garden if its spreading habit of growth is inhibited. The thick roots of madder produce a red

dye that was in great demand for hundreds of years. Different mordants produce varying shades. The tops of the plants can be used for yellow.

Maple, Red *Acer rubrum*

Swedish botanist Peter Kalm, who traveled in North America in the mid-eighteenth century, described the Philadelphians' early use of red maple as a dye. He wrote:

> With the bark they dye both worsted and linen, giving it a dark blue color. For that purpose it was first boiled in water, and some copperas, such as the hatmakers and the shoemakers commonly made use of, is added, before the stuff is put into the boiler. The bark likewise affords a good black ink.

Marigold *Tagetes* varieties

Fresh or dried flower heads are used with a mordant of alum to make a good yellow. The addition of a few black walnut hulls will deepen the color. Cover 1 peck of fresh flower heads, slightly less of the dried ones, with cold water and boil for 1 hour. Strain the liquid into a dye bath. Immerse the wet, mordanted wool in the bath, heat to boiling, and allow to simmer for 1 hour. Rinse and dry the wool in the shade.

Nettle, Stinging *Urtica dioica*

Nettles are usually collected from the wild, but they are sometimes cultivated as companion plantings in the vegetable garden. They originally came from Europe where they were used for making cloth and for food. To produce a green color, cut up 3 pounds of these plants and soak overnight in enough water to cover. Boil for 1 hour and strain the liquid into a bath. Immerse the wool in the lukewarm bath and simmer for 30 minutes. Rinse and dry in the shade.

❀

Oaks (*Quercus*)

Oak, Black   *Quercus velutina*

Early American settlers used the inner bark of this tree to produce bright yellow. Some dyers mordanted the wool in a solution containing alum and cream of tartar. Others considered the mordanting unnecessary and sometimes used oak to set other dyes.

Oak, Red   *Q. rubra*

The inner bark of the red oak can be used to give wool a rose tan color if no mordant is used. Wool will be tan if chrome is used and light brown with an alum mordant. With alum, cotton becomes rose tan.

Oak, White   *Q. alba*

Alum-mordanted wool will take on a dark tan or light brown color if dyed with the inner bark of the white oak. If chrome is used as the mordant, the wool will become khaki.

Onion   *Allium cepa*

The skins of the common cooking onion yield a deep orange. Boil ½ pound of onion skins for 30 minutes and strain the resulting liquid into a bath. Immerse still wet, alum-mordanted wool in the hot dye bath and steep for 1 hour.

Osage Orange   *Maclura pomifera*

This large member of the mulberry family is native to Texas and Arkansas but is hardy in the North. Its numerous fruits, which look like wrinkled green oranges, are quite fragrant when they are fresh. The Navajo Indians used the bark of Osage orange to make a yellow tan dye. With different mordant, yellow, gold, and orange can be produced. An extract of the bark turns alum-mordanted wool a yellow tan and chrome-treated wool a lovely gold.

Parsley, Curly   *Petroselinum crispum*
    All good cooks know that adding one of the curly types of parsley will turn cooking mixtures green. That same culinary herb yields a good yellow green on alum-mordanted wool. Use 2 pounds of fresh parsley leaves and a solution containing 2 ounces of alum.

Pear   *Pyrus communis*
    The leaves of the pear tree produce a yellow tan on wool that has been mordanted in a solution containing 4 ounces of alum and 1 ounce of cream of tartar. Soak 1 pound of leaves in water to cover overnight and boil for 1 hour. Strain the liquid into a bath. Immerse the mordanted wool in the lukewarm bath and simmer for 30 minutes. Rinse and dry in the shade.

Pokeweed   *Phytolacca decandra*
    A colorful weed, with deep reddish purple berries, that has been used as a dye plant for centuries. Peter Kalm wrote:

> When the juice of its berries is put on paper or the like, it dyes it a deep purple, which is as fine as any in the world, and it is a pity that no method has of yet been discovered of making this color last on woolen and linen cloth for it fades very soon.

Although pokeweed is still impractical to use, it deserves a historic spot in the dye garden.

Queen-of-the-meadow   *Filipendula ulmaria*
    This lovely, feathery plant bears a profusion of white flowers. It is especially valuable to the dye gardener, because it can be used to produce three colors—greenish yellow, blue, and black. To produce the yellow, soak the tops of the plants in cold water and then boil them for 1 hour. Strain the liquid into the bath. Immerse the alum-mordanted wool in the dye bath and simmer for 1 hour. Rinse and dry in the shade. For blue, boil the leaves and stalks

[149]

for 2 hours and simmer the wool in the bath along with roots of sorrel. Black will result from a dye bath made of boiled roots.

Rue *Ruta graveolens*
The roots of rue will yield a red dye. Boil the roots for 2 hours and strain the liquid into a bath. Immerse alum-mordanted wool in the dye bath and simmer until the wool assumes a color just slightly darker than the one desired. Rinse and dry in the shade.

Safflower *Carthamus tinctorius*
Native plant of India, an annual, that can be grown from seed. It is sometimes known as bastard saffron, Mexican saffron, and dyer's saffron. The plant yields an oil that can be burned or used for culinary purposes, but the dye is produced from the flower heads. They contain both red and yellow; however, the red is considered more valuable. Alum is the mordant for yellow; red is produced with an alkali mordant. For a good dye, cover 1 peck of flower heads with water, bring to a boil, and simmer for 1 hour. Strain the liquid into a bath. Put the still wet, mordanted wool into the bath and simmer for 1 hour. Rinse and dry in the shade.

St. John's-wort *Artemisia vulgaris*
Hypericum perforatum
An attractive weed found in the East. It usually blooms in midsummer at the Feast of Saint John the Baptist. The plant tops produce yellow on alum-mordanted wool. Simmer for 1 hour plant tops that have been soaked in water overnight. Strain the liquid into the bath. Immerse the still wet, mordanted wool in the warm bath and simmer for 1 hour. Rinse well and dry in the shade.

Sassafras *Sassafras albidum*
S. variifolium
A very decorative tree or shrub that has attractive, mitten-shaped leaves. Its roots yield the bark that is so popular for a medicinal tea in the Midwest and South. Sassafras flowers yield yellow, and

[150]

the roots brown, both with a mordant of alum. If ferrous sulfate and acetic acid are added to the mordant, a rose tan will result.

Sumac   *Rhus glabra*

Although sumac is common enough along the roadside, people seldom recognize it when it is planted in a garden area. It is a decorative, tropical-looking plant that turns to a glorious red in October and bears soft berries that have a sheen over their deep red. Sumac is especially valued by dye gardeners because it is so available, produces several colors, and is itself a mordant. The colonists boiled the leaves and young shoots to extract tannic acid, which they used in mordanting dye materials. The ripe berries yield beige. Soak ½ peck of the berries in water to cover for 12 hours. Boil the mixture for 30 minutes and strain the liquid into a bath. Immerse wet wool or cotton in the lukewarm bath and simmer for 40 minutes. Rinse and dry in the shade. For tan or brown, dry the leaves and young shoots. Soak the cut-up pieces in enough water to cover for 12 hours and then boil the mixture for 30 minutes. Strain the resulting liquid into a bath. Wet the material to be dyed and immerse it in the lukewarm bath and simmer until the color is just slightly darker than the one desired. Rinse and dry in the shade.

Sunflower   *Helianthus* varieties

All sunflowers produce dyes, but the flower of the common one is the largest, so it naturally yields the most dye. Some of the smaller sunflowers are, however, more attractive to grow in most modern gardens. Sunflowers produce a lovely yellow gold on alum-mordanted wool. For 1 pound of wool, boil 2 quarts of dried sunflowers in enough water to cover for 25 minutes. Strain the liquid into a cold water bath of up to 4 gallons. Immerse the mordanted wool in the bath and simmer for 30 minutes. Remove the wool from the dye bath, but do not rinse it. Instead transfer it to a boiling bath containing ⅙ ounce of potassium dichromate and 6–7 tablespoons of vinegar. Boil for 10 minutes. Rinse and dry in the shade.

Sweet Gale *Myrica gale*

A sweet-scented shrub that was popular with the colonists because it could be used to produce three shades of yellow on alum-mordanted wool. We have not included the plant in our plan because we have found that it prefers bog conditions. It is sometimes called bog myrtle. Dyers will probably find it best to collect sweet gale from the wild. Boil fresh leaves in water to cover for 1 hour. Strain the liquid into a bath. For yellow gold, immerse the wet and mordanted wool in the bath and simmer for 45 minutes. The color can be changed to yellow brown if the wool is simmered an additional 15 minutes in the bath to which copper vitriol has been added. Yellow green will result if iron vitriol is substituted for the copper vitriol.

Sweet Woodruff *Asperula odorata*

A charming ground cover and an attractive and fragrant addition to the dye garden. Sweet woodruff, like other members of the madder family, yields red dye from its roots and yellow dye from the tops of the plants. Since this is a small herb, it does not produce as much dye as do larger members of the family. (See Madder, page 146).

Tansy *Tanacetum vulgare*

The yellow tansy flowers are probably the most colorful note in an August garden. The fernlike leaves produce yellow green on alum-mordanted wool if the leaves are harvested before the flowers appear.

Walnut, Black. See Butternut (page 140).

Weld *Reseda luteola*

This native of the Mediterranean, sometimes called Dyer's mignonette, is an ancient annual herb that produces shades of yellow, orange, and gold. The color will be brighter if the entire plant is gathered and used while the flowers are in full bloom, but the dried plant is also useful. Use alum as the mordant for lemon yellow, chrome for golden yellow, alum and tin for orange.

Woad   *Isatis tinctoria*

A very lovely blue dye can be extracted from woad leaves, but the process is complicated and very time-consuming. We include it in our dye garden because of its historical significance and its abundance of yellow flowers in spring. It was widely grown and used in England during the sixteenth and seventeenth centuries when England's production and interests were protected by a guild that fought to keep indigo out of the country. In the early part of the eighteenth century indigo was imported in quantity from the West Indies, and woad's importance diminished.

Zinnia   *Zinnia elegans*

There is an almost barbaric beauty in a thickly planted bed of giant zinnias with smaller varieties growing around them. The blaze of bloom extends until frost finally lays them low. The brilliant flowers of many colors produce only a yellow dye. Mordant 1 pound of wool in a solution of 4 ounces of alum and 1 ounce of cream of tartar. Soak 2 pounds of crushed flowers in water overnight. Boil 1 hour and strain the liquid into a dye bath. Immerse the wool in the bath and simmer for 30 minutes. Rinse and dry in the shade.

7
A Garden of
Medicinal Teas

THE MAIN HOUSE at Caprilands stands on a high knoll. The land drops away from it toward the woods, with the gardens, once pastureland, in between. The gardens are separated from the house and woods by stone walls and are entered by way of stone steps that lead past a row of trees. At the far end of a long grass path that goes past various model gardens is the tea garden. Here we have built a gazebo, or perhaps more truly a garden house, since it does not have the Oriental characteristics of the Victorian tea house. It has been constructed of old barn timber to tie it in with our battered eighteenth-century buildings, and although just erected, it seems to have been there forever.

The tea garden is circular and surrounds the gazebo. Peastone paths lead through the plantings. To provide good drainage, the beds are slightly raised and edged with weathered wood.

The beds in the inner circle contain some of our favorite plants —camomile, sage, rosemary, and calendula. Camomile with its lovely fernlike leaves and flowers gives off the pleasant odor of ripe apples. Calendula, or pot marigold, provides a marvelous display of yellow and gold even after frost destroys most other garden color. Rosemary, the tea to restore memory, is a treasured culinary and decorative herb. The gray green sages, the most valuable and infallible of remedies, provide a marvelous contrast in leaf texture.

In the outer circle are planted the nepetas, calamint, and catnip. Some of the more fragrant mints are also here. Orange mint, which smells so delightful that it is sometimes called eau de cologne, lines one entrance to the tea house and wafts its fresh sweet odor inside.

Against the pasture fence are mints. They are cut and dried for the making of winter teas, so they occupy a large area. The tall apple mint and spearmints are in the back row. Next is the lower-growing peppermint. The tiny creeping Corsican mint, the smallest of all, spreads its moss in crevices of well-placed rocks that protect it from the encroachments of the bigger and bolder members of the family.

The tree teas grow in back of the pasture fence, where they get ample air and sun. These trees for teas include sassafras, with its mitten-shaped leaves, the wild benzoin bush, which blossoms in early May with yellow flowers resembling forsythia, and the black alder, a wild holly, which gives a bonus of red berries in the fall and early winter. A lemony tea is made from the fruits of the common sumac. The young tips of hemlock and black spruce and the inner bark and young tips of red spruce were brewed for tea by the French, the Indians, and the colonists. The bark of dogwood makes a tonic tea.

Shrubs and tall herbs are planted outside the formal beds. Among these is the rugosa rose, appropriate in this tea garden setting because of the very fine brew that can be made from the dried and ground hips. Tall garden angelica has long been considered an excellent remedy for colds, fevers, and attendant ills. It bears spectacular clusters of greenish white flowers. All varieties of sweet bergamot are here, including the wild *B. fistulosa*, which makes the best of the Indian teas, often called Oswego tea. Boneset with its white flowers and the pink-flowered Joe Pye weed are included for their use as stimulants to the stomach, liver, and bowels.

The shrubs in the plantings near the pasture fence include blackberry and raspberry. Around them grow wild strawberries. Most of these are valuable for their leaves rather than their fruits. Nearby is caraway, grown for its seeds, which at one time were widely used in the treatment of hysteria and dyspepsia.

The gazebo is a delightful place to sit and be surrounded by the fragrance and beauty of all the herbs. It is a particularly appropriate place for tea parties. In spring we can look across the fields where cows graze and wild flowers grow. And the scene keeps changing as buttercups and daisies appear and then give way to Joe Pye weed and goldenrod.

HERBS AS MEDICINES

During the course of history all herbs have been examined for their medical properties. Dioscorides, the Greek physician of the first century, experimented during his travels with the Roman armies to expand the realm of materia medica. In the seventeenth

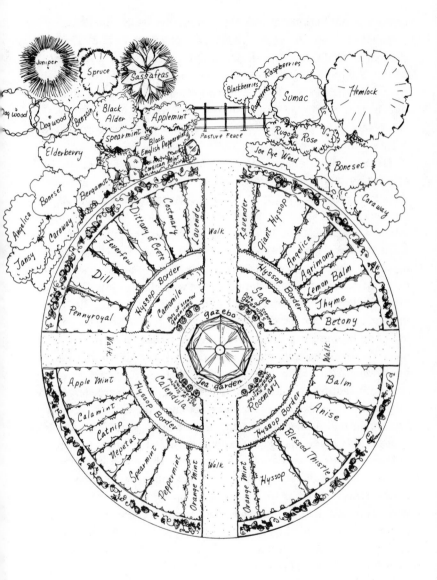

century John Parkinson added to knowledge with his *Theatrum Botanicum*, and Nicholas Culpeper contributed *The English Physician; or An Astrologo-Physical Discourse of the Vulgar Herbs of this Nation*. Medical books dealing with herbs became popular reading in the nineteenth century and often included hand-colored drawings to clarify the appearance of the growing herbs. Many of the plants that we value today for their beauty or scent were early sources of medicines.

The use of herbs as medicines waned with the demise of the apothecary shop and the growth of the drugstore. Today, however, there is a revival of interest in the simple herbal remedies, and some gardeners are examining every aspect of plant lore with fresh vision and application. It is well to remember that the medicinal value of herbs may at times be overstated and herbal remedies depended upon too heavily. It is also possible that through ignorance of botanical nomenclature dangerous plants may easily be mistaken for beneficial ones and used with disastrous results. It is therefore most important that the aspiring herbalist learn the families of herbs and the particular varieties or parts considered medicinal. These plants and parts were called "official" in the early books on herb uses, which were called herbals. It is best to proceed with caution in a field so long neglected. Other gardeners and salesmen whose advice is sought may not know the correct answers. In reading the old herbals remember that there were few records kept or tests made that gave the final results of many treatments.

For all of us who love our herb gardens there is a charm and satisfaction in being able to grow and pick our own remedies and tonics. Our warning is to become familiar with the herbs, know what you are buying, growing, and using. There certainly is therapy in cultivating a garden and joy in producing the medicines of the past, so do not spoil the delight of your medicinal garden by a misuse of the plants.

PLANTS FOR THE
MEDICINAL TEA GARDEN*

Agrimony   *Agrimonia eupatoria*

This decorative plant has beautifully cut leaves and spires of fine yellow flowers. Agrimony was once sought after as a substitute for tea and is today often used as a table beverage in France. Its leaves add a delicate fragrance to regular tea, and they are sometimes boiled for a spring tonic. In his *Herball* written in the sixteenth century, John Gerard said: "A decoction of the leaves is good for them that have naughty livers." According to Culpeper in *Plants of Wisdom*: "It is a most admirable remedy for such whose livers are annoyed by heat or cold. The liver is the former of blood and blood the nourisher of the body and Agrimony a strengthening of the liver." At one time a strong decoction of the roots and the leaves was mixed with honey or sugar and taken to cure skin eruptions caused by "conditions of the blood." Agrimony was thought to be a magic herb during the Middle Ages. It was also supposed to induce heavy sleep when laid under a pillow.

Alder, Black   *Ilex verticillata*
Winterberry

This plant grows in swamps throughout the United States. Both the bark and the glossy scarlet berries are reputed to be therapeutic. The berries, which have a bitter taste, are used for a tonic, for an astringent, and for a worm medicine. The bark has been used in the treatment of fevers, diarrhea, ulcers, and other diseases connected with "a debilitated state of the system." It is given internally and applied locally in the form of a wash or poultice. Teas may be made by adding 1 cup of boiling water to 1 teaspoon of either the bark or the berries.

---

* Includes some plants not shown in plot plan.

[159]

Angelica   *Angelica archangelica*

Angelica is sometimes called the Holy Ghost Plant and Saint Michael's Plant, since it blooms on his day (May 8) in many parts of the world. It is a tall and dramatic plant with large clusters of greenish flowers. Today the plant is used primarily as a flavoring agent in candies and liqueurs and for the decoration of birthday cakes and Christmas coffee rings, particularly in France and Germany. A really tasty tea can be prepared by infusion of either the fresh or the dried leaves. It is particularly good when sweetened with honey. The whole plant is said to have stimulant and tonic qualities. It has been used as a remedy for colds, coughs, pleurisy, flatulence, rheumatism, and fevers. Gerard even tells us that "it cureth the bitings of mad dogs and all other venomous beasts." The aromatic seeds sometimes flavor liqueurs; the root is often powdered for medicinal uses.

Anise   *Pimpinella anisum*

Anise is an herb of very ancient fame. In biblical times it was used in the payment of taxes. The Romans used it to cure indigestion: they made a cake of it that was served after meals of rich foods. More recently anise tea has been considered beneficial in the treatment of bronchitis, asthma, colic, and nausea. A teaspoon of leaves is brewed in 1 cup of boiling water for 30 minutes. The same hot brew, consumed before retiring, is taken for indigestion. An oil extracted from the seeds is of great commercial value in today's market, in the preparation of anisette, and for that familiar licorice flavoring.

Bachelors Button   *Centaurea cyanus*

This plant was named after a centaur whose wounds were cured by a cornflower. Varieties were known in Turkey and the Near East as Sultan's flower. John Parkinson wrote of it: "We in these dayes do chiefly use . . . [*Cyanus vulgaris*] as a cooling cordiall and commended by some to be a remedy not only against the plague and pestilentiall diseases, but against the poison of Scorpions and Spiders."

Benzoin Bush   *Lindera benzoin*
Spice Bush

In the early spring woods this lovely shrub resembles forsythia, although the flowers are a more brownish yellow. It is so abundant in the eastern part of the States that one can pick it without restraint. Its oily, aromatic berries are bright red and appear after the blossoms have gone, in April. The leaves, twigs, bark, and berries all have a strong aromatic taste. Its reputation with the colonists and other pioneers was great as a relaxing and tasteful tea. In 1796 André Michaux, a French botanist, wrote of his travels through the wilderness:

> I had supped the previous evening on tea made from the shrub called Spicewood. A handful of young twigs or branches is set to boil and after it has boiled a quarter of an hour, sugar is added and it is drunk like tea . . . this beverage restores strength, and it had that effect for I was very tired when I arrived.

Bergamot   *Monarda didyma*
Oswego Tea   *M. fistulosa*
Bee Balm

Monarda didyma, the red-flowered monarda, was known to the Indians and the early settlers, who made a hot beverage of the leaves. The minty-flavored brew was called Oswego tea because the plant grew profusely around Oswego, New York.

M. fistulosa, which has purple flowers, makes a tea that is said to be a sedative, but the red-flowered variety has the most fragrant foliage and is generally preferred for tea. The leaves of both plants are infused in boiling water for 15 minutes.

Betony   *Betonica officinalis*
                                    Stachys officinalis
                                    S. betonica

Betony has spikes of lovely purple flowers in June and July. It was once so highly prized for its many cures that it inspired an

[161]

old saying, "Better sell your coat and buy Betony." A pleasantly warm and somewhat astringent tea with a slightly bitter taste is made from the dried leaves. It must be brewed for 20 minutes to bring out the flavor. The root was considered an emetic and a purgative.

Birch, Sweet   *Betula lenta*
   Infusions of the sweet birch leaves have been prescribed for gout, rheumatism, dropsy, and cutaneous diseases. A tea made of the inner bark is said to quell fevers.

Blackberry   *Rubus* varieties
   The "official" part of the blackberry, that part recommended by the apothecaries, is the root. The product extracted from the roots with either boiling water or alcohol is used in the treatment of dysentery, but there are others who say that blackberry jelly is also good for "summer complaint." It is a pleasant remedy.

Boneset   *Eupatorium perfoliatum*
   The curious name came from the plant's importance in the treatment of a fever in which the pain was so great that it was called break bone fever. It was once commonly brewed as a remedy for all fevers, although some say that it is also important as a stimulant to the stomach. In small doses it becomes a tonic.

Calamint   *Calamintha*
                                                       Satureja calamintha
   An attractive plant with deep green leaves and whorls of tiny blue or lilac flowers. Either the green or the dried leaves make a tasty tea that is sometimes useful in the treatment of fevers. It is a pleasant tisane or bedtime tea.

Calendula   *Calendula officinalis*
Pot Marigold   (or varieties)
   One of the most brilliant and colorful beds in our tea garden is planted with pot marigolds. It provides us with a mass of yellow

[162]

and gold throughout the summer and fall. The lovely flowers were reputed to heal a disturbed heart, better the complexion and disposition, and speed healing from accidents. According to Culpeper, "They strengthen the heart exceedingly and are very expulsive and a little less effectual in the small pox and measles than saffron." We use the leaves and blossoms in salad and make a tea of dried leaves, adding mint leaves.

Camomile, German *Matricaria chamomilla*

Anthemis nobilis, the true or Roman camomile, is grown largely in England, where it thrives. In this country it has, for the most part, been supplanted by *M. chamomilla*, which has similar properties and is my preference for tea. German camomile has a special bed in our garden, for it is a very special herb, with attractive and mossy leaves in spring. As we walk through the paths bordered with it or where its spreading fernlike leaves are filling in as ground cover, the odor of ripe apples rises. Dried camomile flowers make a good and aromatic tea that is said to be a nerve tonic. It is taken for insomnia and other nervous disorders. Early herbals also suggest its use for jaundice, toothache, and snakebite. Many call it a beauty herb because it is good for washing blond hair.

Caraway *Carum carvi*

A tea for indigestion and for flatulent colic is made of caraway seeds boiled in water. It was widely used as a carminative cordial and for the treatment of dyspepsia, hysteria, and other disorders. The oil extracted from the seeds flavors cordials.

Catnip *Nepeta cataria*
Catmint

Catnip, which grows wild in much of the United States, was introduced from England and has naturalized. It has been used as a tea in both countries, liked as much for its flavor as for its many reputed medical virtues—to soothe the nerves, relieve fevers, ward off colds, quiet restlessness, and dispel nightmares. The root, when chewed, is said to make the most retiring and gentle people quarrelsome!

Comfrey   *Symphytum officinale*

A long row of the huge and prolific comfreys among the trees in the grove makes a background for the tea garden. It grows so thick and fast that smaller and weaker plants are easily overrun unless the plants are constantly cut and the seedlings dug and transplanted to keep it within bounds. The roots of comfrey are generally thought to be medicinal, but the Russians and the Polish use both the leaves and the roots to speed the healing of broken bones. The long, green, hairy leaves may be dried for a tea. They are best when combined with other herbs, like mint, to improve the flavor. Leaves of comfrey drying in our open shed give it the appearance of a tobacco barn.

Costmary   *Chrysanthemum balsamita*

This is a fragrant and decorative plant that Culpeper said "is astringent to the stomach, strengthening to the liver and all inward parts." The whole plant or the roots may be used. For an old remedy for catarrhal conditions, dried leaves are infused in boiling water for 15 minutes. The tasty tea is drunk twice daily.

Dill   *Anethum graveolens*

A tall, feathery-leaved plant that is a must for the tea garden for the sedative that is made by steeping its seeds in hot water. In earlier times the seeds were used in witchcraft.

Dittany of Crete   *Origanum dictamnus*

A relative of marjoram, this lovely, gray-leaved, tender perennial is a most decorative, though minute, addition to the herb border, where it is sometimes used as an edging. The plant is named for its place of origin, Mount Dictamnus in Greece, where legend has it that wild goats ate it to free themselves from the hurt of hunters' arrows. Tea is made from the flowering heads, which resemble those of hops. The brew is an old-fashioned tisane used for indigestion.

Dogwood *Cornus* varieties

All of the native dogwoods may be used for aromatic tonics and astringents. The infusion is made by pouring boiling water on an ounce of powdered bark. The normal dose is from one to two ounces.

Elderberry *Sambucus canadensis*

Flowers of elderberry are a gentle excitant but are seldom used except externally as a poultice. The berries are diaphoretic and are used in treatments for gout, rheumatism, and dropsy.

Fennel *Foeniculum vulgare*
(all varieties)

Fennel raises tall umbrels of yellow flowers among the herbs. Its tea made of the seeds has an ancient reputation as a restorative and a cure for children's stomachaches.

Feverfew *Chrysanthemum parthenium*

Lovely, lasting heads of white flowers appear in the feverfew bed of the tea garden. A tea made of these flowers is reputed to relieve nervous pains, neuralgia, earache, and rheumatism.

Geraniums, Rose *Pelargonium graveolens*

Rose geraniums are an attractive part of the tea planting both for the beauty of their unusual leaves and for their sweet scent. Use either fresh or dried leaves; we prefer the green ones. To make a fragrant tea, try 2 bags of China tea, 3 rose geranium leaves, and 6 cloves. Brew this for a least 10 minutes; 20 to 30 minutes may not be too long. Reduce with hot water if it becomes too strong. Serve hot or over ice. Garnish with a fragrant leaf from the plant.

Hemlock *Tsuga*

For a spring tonic, steep the young tips of hemlock in boiling water and sweeten the brew with maple sugar. This was a remedy used by the early pioneers.

Hyssop *Hyssopus officinalis*

An attractive plant with boxlike leaves and spikes of dark blue, pink, or white flowers. Both leaves and flowers are reputed to have medicinal properties. A tea made of the fresh green tops is an old-fashioned cure for rheumatism. An infusion of the dried flowers, sweetened with honey, was drunk for "debility of the chest."

Indian Squaw Bush *Rhus trilobata*
High Bush Cranberry

A handsome shrub, with bright red berries. A decoction of its roots has long been used for the treatment of cramps.

Joe Pye Weed *Eupatorium purpureum*

Pink-flowered eupatorium fills our swamps and roadsides with beauty in the early fall. Legends have it that the plant was named for a famous healer and that Joe Pye was the name of a fever that the Indians dreaded—probably typhoid. The weed was the most effective aid in checking the fever.

Juniper *Juniperus communis*

The mature blue black berries of this evergreen are primarily used ih flavoring gin and a French beer. The Laplanders, however, brewed them for a medicinal tea. The berries are a frosty gray when they first appear.

Lady's Mantle *Alchemilla vulgaris*
Our Lady's Mantle

We are glad to have an excuse to include Lady's mantle in the medicinal tea garden, for its low growth and fluted, grayish leaves are decorative in all seasons. The flowers, which look like yellow baby's breath, cut and dry well for winter bouquets. The dried and crushed leaves make a medicinal tea popular in Switzerland for many minor ailments and in childbirth. Its virtues are much like those of camomile.

Lavender   *Lavandula* varieties

Lavender teas have long been out of fashion, but they have in the past been recommended for headaches caused by too much sun and for nervous tension. Parkinson said the dried flowers were effective "to comfort and dry up the moisture of a cold braine." We have planted two of these lovely and fragrant bushes at one entrance to the gazebo where we brush by them and carry their sweet scent inside.

Lemon Balm   *Melissa officinalis*

"Let a sirup made with the juice of it and sugar be kept in every gentlewoman's house to relieve the weak stomachs and sick bodies of their poor sickly neighbors."—Culpeper

"It causeth the mind and heart to become merry and revives the heart faintings and swoonings—especially on such who are overtaken in sleep and drives away all troubles and thoughts out of the mind arising from melancholy or black choler. It is very good to help digestion and open obstructions of the brain."—Seraphic

A tea that has more recently been recommended for feverish colds can be made from either the fresh or the dried leaves. Pour 1 pint of boiling water over 1 ounce of the herb and allow it to infuse for 10 minutes. At Caprilands we make a lemon balm punch that is very popular, even though we are not sure of its therapeutic value. Marinate 1 cup of green leaves in 1 gallon of dry sauterne for 2 hours or more. Slice lemons and limes into the wine. Add 1 quart of vermouth. Serve over ice and garnish with small marigolds.

Lemon Verbena   *Lippia citriodora*

One of the sweetest of fragrant herbs is a tree from the volcanic highlands of Guatemala and South America. It grows fast and furiously during the spring and summer to make up for its poor appearance in the winter and to produce many cups of long green leaves for an excellent tea. These may be harvested and dried for winter use. In France the tea is called *vervain* and is one of the most popular tisanes.

Mint (*Mentha*)

The bed of mints helps to turn the medicinal tea garden into one of the coolest and most fragrant spots.

Apple Mint   *Mentha rotundifolia*
The soft, gray green leaves and pale pink to purple flowers make apple mint a handsome addition to the tea garden. Its dried leaves make a distinctive tea alone or in combination with other herbs. It is the base of Caprilands tea, which also includes rosemary, sage, thyme, marjoram, pot marigold, and camomile. Apple mint was once thought to be a cure for epilepsy.

Orange Mint   *M. citrata*
Bergamot Mint
In early spring orange mint adds a special contrast to the appearance of the tea garden because it has a reddish purple color. The leaves turn green in summer. Either the fresh or the dried leaves add an interesting flavor to Oriental teas, and those made only from the dried leaves have a very pleasant taste, odor, and color. An especially pleasing brew can be made by combining 1 quart of dried orange mint leaves, the grated and dried rind of 1 orange and 1 lemon, 8 teaspoons of commercial tea, 1 teaspoon of ground cloves, and 1 cup of dried pot marigold petals. The mixture can be stored in airtight containers for some time.

Pennyroyal   *M. pulegium*
A creeping and spreading plant that makes an attractive ground cover. It has lovely blue blossoms. Tea made of the leaves benefits the sinuses, but in the past it had a great reputation for curing spasms, jaundice, and "pains of the head due to colds."

Peppermint *M. piperita vulgaris*

The English black peppermint, a handsome and dark plant with purplish blue flowers, is the most flavorful of the peppermints. An aromatic, warm tea with a hint of coolness is made of the dried leaves. This has been used to avert or correct nausea, to treat heat prostration, and to relieve stomach and bowel complaints.

Spearmint *M. spicata*

A green plant with crinkly and spearlike leaves, spearmint is the most popular of all members of this large family. Tea can be made of the dried leaves alone, or they can be mixed with one of Chinese origin. Spearmint tea is sometimes used for colic, nervous headaches, and diarrhea.

Nepeta *Nepeta species*

Nepeta mussinii, N. 'Six Hills Giant', *N. grandiflora, N. macrantha, N. nuda,* and *N. reticulata,* all members of the catnip family, are very attractive garden plants that bloom until fall if cut back after the first flowering. They bear purplish blue flowers (except *macrantha,* which is blue) in spikes. Teas made of their dried leaves are said to soothe the nerves.

Nettle, Stinging *Urtica dioica*

Although this is an unpleasant plant to run against, for the leaves may cause itching or a rash, it is one of the most highly recommended natural medicines. It contains large amounts of vitamin A. Green nettle tea, made with the addition of comfrey leaves, both of which have been run through the blender, makes a healthful drink to improve vision and to add gloss to the hair. It may be served either hot or cold.

Raspberry, Wild *Rubus*

Raspberry fruit is fragrant and cooling. Combined with white vinegar, it makes a liquor that can be diluted with water and used to treat fevers, scurvy, and sore throat. Gerard said, "The fruit is good to be given them that have weake and queasie stomackes."

Rose, Rugosa   *Rosa rugosa*
The rose seed cases called rose hips, are used to make a very pleasant tea. The addition of honey and a slice of lemon or orange improves the flavor.

Rosemary   *Rosmarinus officinalis*
Rosemary is a gracious plant no matter what the setting. In the gazebo tea garden we have our "official" plant, that is, an old plant that has reached five feet, surrounded by one-year-olds that the small and shrublike. These plants give us enough cuttings for our favorite rosemary tea, which is a very ancient usage and famous for restoring the memory. Gerard said, "Rosemary is a remedy against stuffing of the head that cometh through coldness of the brain."

Safflower   *Carthamus tinctorius*
American saffron is a decorative thistle with a yellow blossom. Yellow plants were generally supposed by Culpeper and others to be marked by the Creator to show what their mission would be. Because they were yellow, they were used to cure "the yellows," now known as jaundice. All golden flowers were called plants of the sun and partook of some of its virtues—bringing joy to the melancholy and good spirits to the depressed. Safflower tea is made from safflower flowers alone or in combination with the leaves of other plants, often mint. It adds a yellow glow to some of the paler brews.

Sage (Blue)   *Salvia officinalis*
Common Sage
The gray leaves of garden sage are decorative and add much interest to the garden, and the flowers attract bees and humming-birds. All the herbalists believed the virtues of sage were endless.

It is reputed to bring a long and happy life. It is also recommended to turn gray hair dark and to be good for the teeth and gums. According to Culpeper, "Jupiter claims this and bids me tell you it is good for the liver and to breed blood. Sage is of excellent use to help the memory, warming and quickening the senses. It is much commended against the stitch or pains in the side coming of wind. . . ." Sage makes such a good-tasting tea of rich color that the Chinese once preferred it to their own. Use 2 teaspoons of dried leaves to a small earthenware pot of boiling water. It must be brewed quite a bit longer than ordinary tea. An excellent brew can also be made by combining the leaves of sage, thyme, and rosemary

Sage, Pineapple   *S. rutilans*

Pineapple sage is grown in our herbal tea garden primarily for its delightful odor, attractive growth, and brilliant red flowers in the fall, Tea made of the green leaves of this plant is not very flavorful, but it has a fragrant breath of pineapple. The leaf is an attractive garnish.

Sassafras   *Sassafras*

Tea made from the top of the root near the trunk is an old standby as a spring tonic. Unlike most other teas, this one must be boiled a long time.

Spruce, Black   *Picea mariana*

The young tips of the tree and the inner bark make a beer that is said to be a very good spring tonic. The pioneers made this beverage.

Strawberry, Wild   *Fragaria vesca*

From Parkinson's *Kitchen Garden*:

> The leaves of Strawberries are always used among other herbes in cooling drinks, as also in lotions and gargles for

the mouth and throate; the rootes are sometimes added to make it more effectuall and withall somewhat the more binding. The berries themselves are often brought to the table as a reare service, whereunto claret wine, creame or milke is added with sugar as every one liketh.

The water distilleth of the berries is good for the passions of the heart, caused by the perturbation of the spirits, being either drunk alone, or in wine; and maketh the heart merry.

Some do hold that the water helpeth to clense the face from spots, and to add some clearenesse to the skinne.

Sumac, Smooth   *Rhus glabra*

Sumac berries are an astringent and a refrigerant. Their infusion has been recommended as a cooling drink for fibral complaints and a pleasant gargle for inflammation or ulceration of the throat. They make a kind of lemony tea.

Tansy   *Tanacetum vulgare*

Tansy was one of the most important medical herbs in the early American garden. Its green or dried leaves made an excellent cordial tonic used to aid digestion, to relieve rheumatic troubles, to soothe nerves, and as an antidote to poison ivy. The yellow, buttonlike blossoms were brewed into a bitter tea that was given to children to bring out the measles. The fernlike leaves are very aromatic and form the base for our moth preventive. This is a favorite plant for gardens with a lot of space and where something can be provided for it to lean against. It can, however, be a menace in a small garden.

Thistle, Blessed   *Carduus benedictus*
                                             Cnicus benedictus

Tea made of ½ ounce of thistle leaves to 1 pint of boiling water is taken as a mild tonic for the stomach. The same preparation has been used to treat fevers, because it produces copious perspiration. Camomile tea is now preferred for this purpose.

Thyme   *Thymus serpyllum*

Thyme is a vigorous, spreading, low plant with showers of lovely white flowers in August. This European plant was introduced by the colonists and has now naturalized. An infusion of the leaves has been recommended for colic, melancholia, sore throat, insomnia, nightmares, and hangovers!

Veronica   *Veronica officinalis*
Speedwell

The tall spikes of blue flowers produced by veronica in late summer are a handsome addition to any garden. Both the seeds and the leaves have been valued highly for their medicinal properties. At one time it was known as *thea de l'Europe*. The medicinal tea has been used as a strengthening medicine, for rheumatism, hemorrhages, and skin diseases. It was once a universal substitute for regular tea.

Wintergreen   *Gaultheria procumbens*

Partridgeberry and teaberry are other names given this charming creeping plant with shiny leathery leaves, white flowers, and red berries. The berries are a favorite food of the birds, and the colonists used the leaves for tea. As a medicine, wintergreen was used for colds, fever, and rheumatic pains. The green leaves must be steeped for at least a day before the right flavor is produced.

Index